# CHRISTIANITY

*a brief introduction*

## Charles E. Farhadian

**BakerAcademic**
*a division of Baker Publishing Group*
Grand Rapids, Michigan

Lovingly dedicated to
*Jeanette Farhadian*

—៣្ក—

Published by Baker Academic
a division of Baker Publishing Group
PO Box 6287, Grand Rapids, MI 49516-6287
www.bakeracademic.com

Printed in the United States of America

Library of Congress Cataloging-in-Publication Data
Names: Farhadian, Charles E., 1964– author.
Title: Christianity : a brief introduction / Charles E. Farhadian.
Description: Grand Rapids, Michigan : Baker Academic, a division of Baker Publishing
    Group, 2020. | Includes index.
Identifiers: LCCN 2020018366 | ISBN 9781540960221 (paperback) | ISBN
    9781540963574 (casebound)
Subjects: LCSH: Christianity—Essence, genius, nature.
Classification: LCC BT60 .F37 2020 | DDC 230—dc23
LC record available at https://lccn.loc.gov/2020018366

In keeping with biblical principles of creation stewardship, Baker Publishing Group advocates the responsible use of our natural resources. As a member of the Green Press Initiative, our company uses recycled paper when possible. The text paper of this book is composed in part of post-consumer waste.

green press INITIATIVE

20   21   22   23   24   25   26          7   6   5   4   3   2   1

# CONTENTS

# PREFACE

B ooks are often born from conversations. This one was. On a walk with Jim Kinney, executive vice president at Baker Publishing Group, I shared my interest in writing something on "world Christianity" in order to add my own ideas to the important conversation about this relatively new field of study. On further thought, turning "Christianity" into "world Christianity" seemed artificial. Isn't Christianity already global without the redundancy of attaching "world" or "global" to it? Calling it "world Christianity" or "global Christianity" would be unnecessary since its transnational connections are part and parcel of the faith, something already written indelibly into its DNA. Christianity was at its inception "global," beginning with Jewish communities and then burgeoning into gentile regions and beyond. This means that rather than being a stagnant set of doctrines, Christianity is a movement, whose final destination is hinterland, suburbia, and urban centers. It is the nature of Christianity to be worldwide, to extend itself beyond its current boundaries. That expansion has made Christianity a global religion.

The purpose of this book is straightforward: to provide an accessible introduction to Christianity, without getting sidetracked by following too many bunny trails of debate that have wracked the faith since its inception. Some of those conflicts will be noted, since they are crucial to the way that Christianity has been shaped, but this is not a conflict-driven book. Rather, the book lays out a clear and generous view of Christianity, noting the influences that have shaped the religion through the centuries. By "generous" I mean that I pitch Christianity as a broad movement that consists of Roman Catholic, Eastern Orthodox, and Protestant expressions. It is important to recognize that while these three streams of Christianity account for the vast majority of Christians, they are not representative of all forms of the faith.

Christian readers will find themselves at home in these pages. They will recognize the key concepts of Christianity and locate themselves within its broad themes. And those new to the faith or without any knowledge of it will find a friendly approach that honors readers' intelligence without being overly academic. What makes Christianity tick? What is so compelling about it? Why ought we to be interested in Christianity? I will answer these questions and more in this book.

Over the past years, there has been interminable talk about Christianity, as both help and hindrance. Christianity, at once blamed for social conflict and embraced as revitalizing individuals and cultures, is such a massive religion that almost anything one says about it could be true, at least in some place or time. One thing is absolutely correct: Christianity, like other religions, is not simply a set of doctrines or practices. Rather, Christianity is deeply connected to everything in life, from how one understands the cosmos, to how one navigates one's inner life, to whom one marries and how one treats others.

Views of the body, the natural world, politics, economics, ethics, one's mind, ambitions, suffering, anxiety, and hope are profoundly shaped and given meaning and purpose by Christianity. While coverage of all these topics is impossible in such a few pages, this book strikes a balance between breadth and depth, without succumbing to either superficiality or the hedged-in, intractable tensions within Christianity.

On several occasions, while traveling internationally, I have been asked variations of the same question. It goes something like this: "What religion are you, Catholic, Methodist, or Lutheran?" What an incongruous question, since these three "religions" are actually the same religion—they are all forms of Christianity. The word "ecumenism" was a more popular term in the past, but it still conveys an important insight about Christianity. "Ecumenism" means the "whole household of God." To be ecumenical means to affirm the church's unity above denominational lines. Unfortunately, this does not always work out well on the ground, but many Christians do recognize that Christianity is essentially one, made up of many expressions. That is to say, anyone who accepts the basic affirmations of Christianity is Christian, whether they are Roman Catholic, Methodist, Lutheran, or one of the hundreds, probably even thousands, of denominations of Christianity. This book presents the parameters of Christianity that define the faith for all Christians.

My hope is that anyone—Christian or otherwise—can read this book and gain an appreciation for the largest religion in the world. Part of the uniqueness of this work is my purposeful departure from focusing exclusively on the Global North. My hope is that the interest of Christians reading this book will be piqued and refreshed by its global viewpoint. Practitioners of other religious traditions will find here a concise study of Christianity, not just its Western perspectives.

My understanding of Christianity comes from years of study, personal experience, and interactions with Christians. I teach world religions at Westmont College, a Christian liberal arts college located in Santa Barbara, California, where I compare religions such as Hinduism, Buddhism, Jainism, Sikhism, Shinto, Taoism, and Confucianism. I also teach Christian missiology, the study of the sending of the Christian church into the world to share the good news of Jesus Christ, where I emphasize the cultural and social shifts that occur when communities become Christian. Interpreting those changes within Christianity requires the ability to see the tradition from within and without—that is, to understand Christianity through the eyes of the believer as well as from the vantage point of an outsider to the faith. So I write both as an insider to Christianity and as one who can see the tradition from outside itself, at least in terms of comparing it with other religions.

For more than three decades I have visited Christians outside of the Global North. Experiences of learning from Christians from Africa, Asia, Latin America, and the Pacific continue to be a source of great inspiration to me personally and, at times, serve as a corrective to what I often see as a far too abstract way of seeing the faith. Any worthwhile interpretation of Christianity must strike a balance between the abstract (e.g., theological) and concrete (e.g., ethnographic). I seek to uphold that balance.

First, I want to thank Jim Kinney of Baker Academic for helping me to lucidly communicate the ideas in this book. I want to thank my students at Westmont College for their enthusiasm for learning and exploring ideas within Christianity and other religions. A debt of gratitude goes to Gina A. Zurlo and Todd M. Johnson, codirectors of the Center for the Study of Global Christianity at Gordon-Conwell Theological Seminary. Thank you to the countless Christians I have met in Africa, Asia, Latin America, and the Pacific, since they have taught me more than books alone can convey about the faith. I also thank my wife, Katherine, and sons, Gabriel and Gideon, for their patience and love as I worked on this book. Finally, I want to thank my mom, Jeanette Farhadian, now ninety-four years old, whose bold witness continues to remind me of the seriousness of the state of our current and future lives—the state of our souls. Little else matters other than knowing God the Father, Son, and Holy Spirit. This book is lovingly dedicated to her. All mistakes are mine.

# INTRODUCTION

How would you characterize Christianity? What do others say? Everyone has an opinion about Christianity. It is the largest religion in the world and has the broadest global reach. What began with a motley group of around a dozen quite unextraordinary people has burgeoned into nearly every conceivable social, economic, and cultural grouping in the world. Dating back more than two millennia, Christianity's expansion into cultures has left indelible marks worldwide, leaving in its wake great transformations.

The religion of celibate monks, CEOs of multinational corporations, homeless persons, and those of every other social, cultural, political, and economic category, Christianity has been used to justify at once horrendous exploits (e.g., the Crusades, South African apartheid) as well as acts of sacrificial living (e.g., Mother Teresa, Martin Luther King Jr.). Each of these ways of interpreting and living out Christianity was made by believers convinced that Christianity inspired specific responses to the world's ills. Yet others assert that Christianity is fundamentally about right belief—not primarily about action—that is, an affirmation of a particular set of doctrines about God and the world.

Christianity has been used and misused in countless ways. Think of the movements and activities done in the name of Christianity: the Inquisition, the Ku Klux Klan, the global rise of religious nationalism that despise secular governments, and Christian militias throughout the world whose main objective is to establish sovereign Christian states in their regions. Several messianic movements have blended local political aspirations with Christianity, often in violent ways. One of the most colorful armed revolutionary Christian insurgent groups was God's Army, which, beginning in the late 1990s, conducted guerrilla actions along the Thailand-Burma border in opposition to the military junta of Myanmar (Burma). God's Army was directed by Karen twin boys Johnny and Luther Htoo, believed to be animated by supernatural power. They were twelve years old at the time. The boy leaders combined biblical passages with desires for Karen political liberation. Many other similar movements, where elements of Christianity are employed for social and political ends, and sometimes with violence, have erupted throughout history.

Is Christianity an instrument of political revolutions, pacifism, cultural destruction, enlightenment, and social subjugation, or the source of everything good that we experience? Is Christianity a hindrance or a help to human flourishing? To be sure, the history of Christianity is uneven in terms of making the world a better or a worse place. What is done "in the name of Christ" is not always of Christ. Whatever one thinks of these matters, the impact of Christianity worldwide ought to capture our attention. What is it that compels people to become Christians despite having to pay a high price for that change? Why would people become Christian even in the face of knowing that they will be harmed or lose their job or family? What would drive Christians to maintain their faith even in the midst of intense hardship? Something attracts people to Christian faith.

When writing this book, I thought about photography, not only because photography is a hobby of mine but also because I found the basic principles of photography to be an effective way to frame my writing. Photography inspires me to see the world differently—for instance, to see shadows and lines and colors in ways I had overlooked before. The lessons from photography are applicable to understanding Christianity.

What makes a compelling photo? First, there is light. Light is fundamental to excellent photography. It is the most important element when photographing a compelling image. But a photographer can capture too much light or too little, making the image too bright or too dark. Likewise, in this book I allow enough light to shine on our subject matter—Christianity—so that it is well illuminated, but I avoid overexposing or underexposing it. We want to see enough detail without letting those details distract from the subject matter.

Second, color helps create a mood of an image—for instance, where blue ocean water in the image conveys a peaceful, tranquil feeling in the viewer. A compelling photograph often captures all possible color tones in the image. In the same way, this book captures something of the breadth of Christianity—as many tones, colorations, and expressions as possible within its few pages.

Third, a great photograph freezes the image at just the right moment. Timing is crucial. In fact, an image might be weaker on any of the other measures mentioned here, but with perfect timing the photo has the potential to be superb. In a similar manner, I have had to decide what moments to capture in Christianity. Christianity looks different in first-century Palestine, eighth-century Ethiopia, sixteenth-century Germany, and twenty-first-century Mexico. No photographer or writer can capture all moments.

Fourth, photographers use composition to frame their subjects, emphasizing the elements the photographer desires for the viewer to see. A well-composed image will grab the viewer's attention. Using excellent composition, even a still image will communicate a sense of dynamism. Composition includes background, middle ground, and foreground that together give depth to an image. What is included in the image and what is excluded? Each photograph is an exercise in selective seeing. Likewise, in each chapter I present Christianity in contexts where some elements are backgrounded and others are foregrounded. I will argue that it is impossible to extract Christianity entirely from any context—there is no such thing as a "pure" Christianity. I will say more about this in chapter 1. Similar to photography, some features of Christianity will be left out of our image.

A final feature of photography that helped frame my writing of this book and that is related to composition is the concept of *bokeh*. The term *bokeh*, the Japanese word that refers to the aesthetic quality of the blur produced when parts of the image are out of focus, contributes to a photograph's appeal since it draws our attention to the subject matter, be it a flower petal, a massive building, or the smile on an infant's face. Just like in photography, where the subject is never without context and the background enhances the focal point, so too with Christianity—Christianity is always connected to an environment, an ecology of cultures, societies, and historical moments. In this book, I strike a balance between the focal point of Christianity and the background blur of context; that is, my aim is to foreground the universal elements within Christianity and its various contexts.

The single question that runs like a thread throughout the chapters of this book is, What is Christianity? I wrote this book with non-Christians in mind, so I avoid the technical jargon prevalent in academic theology and biblical studies. However, this book is also written for Christians with holes in their knowledge about Christianity, with the hope that they will see a compelling image of the breadth and depth of Christianity worldwide. To respect you, the reader, I strike a balance between insider and outsider perspectives, recognizing that objectivity is impossible when it comes to religion.

This book counteracts many misconceptions and misrepresentations about Christianity. When Christianity is seen, for example, as a Western religion, or Christians are perceived as illogical, or when Christianity is taken to mean following a laundry list of rules, then it is time for clarification. These and other myths need to be dispelled. When the background of politics, economics, or a particular culture gets foregrounded in one's interpretation of Christianity, then we need to reposition Christianity in order to see it plainly. Another reason for this book is that we need a clear presentation of the faith that does not succumb to a politicization of Christianity that equates it with a particular political party or economic system. The fact that Christianity is a religion that spans the globe reminds us that it has made its home in a variety of contexts.

This book is organized around several queries, each geared toward illuminating an aspect of the question that forms its spine, What is Christianity? Most definitions of Christianity focus on Jesus of Nazareth. A quick Internet search yields these definitions of Christianity: "the religion based on the person and teachings of Jesus of Nazareth, or its belief and practices";[1] "the religion derived from

1. "Christianity," Lexico, https://www.lexico.com/en/definition/christianity.

Jesus Christ, based on the Bible as sacred scripture, and professed by Eastern, Roman Catholic, and Protestant bodies";[2] and "an Abrahamic monotheistic religion based on the life and teachings of Jesus of Nazareth."[3] Undoubtedly, Jesus of Nazareth plays a crucial role in any definition of Christianity. Without Jesus, there would be no such thing as Christianity. Yet Christianity means more than the life and teaching of Jesus of Nazareth; for instance, there is movement (mission), Scripture (Bible), gathering (church), and celebration and learning (worship).

Chapter 1, "Who Are Christians?" lays out the parameters of Christian orthodoxy, which was defined by the early church's reading of the Bible. Rather than being a list of propositional truths, "Christian" is both a noun, as a thing to be studied, and an adjective, a modifier that creates new meaning, such as "Christian singing." Here we will read about the critically important concept of the Triune God, envisioned as one substance in three persons, Father, Son, and Holy Spirit.

A fruitful way to understand any religious movement is to see it from an insider's perspective. Therefore, in the first chapter we will overhear what early Christians said about themselves. We will discover that early Christians formed a new community united by the Triune God and marked by kinship language (e.g., "brother" and "sister") that reflected the depth of a new kind of relationship established among once disparate people. These reconfigured communities, centered on Jesus Christ and empowered by the Holy Spirit, were described in the Bible as assemblies where "there is neither Jew nor Gentile, neither slave nor free, nor is there male and female, for you are all one in Christ Jesus" (Gal. 3:28). Certainly, Christianity had a leveling effect on social relations.

Members of this new community who followed the Way, the Jesus movement, came from all walks of life; they were male and female, educated and uneducated. All of them *became* Christians—they converted, changed their thinking and course of life. That turning—or

2. "Christianity," Merriam-Webster, https://www.merriam-webster.com/dictionary/Christianity.
3. "Christianity," Wikipedia, https://en.wikipedia.org/wiki/Christianity.

conversion—involved not only their self-understanding as individuals and communities but also their wider contexts. What elements of their cultures would remain a part of their lives to be transformed, and what features would fall out entirely?

The relationship between Christianity and culture is illuminated in this section, where I argue that nothing is Christian at the start. Rather, things *become* Christian as they are reoriented under the revelation of Jesus Christ. The chapter also takes a look at statements of shared belief of the Christian community, called creeds, which reflect the historical continuity of Christian belief. Creeds unite the church around the world, as they are agreed-upon affirmations of Christian orthodoxy.

Chapter 2, "Where Are Christians?" provides a springboard to investigate both the expansion of Christianity and the nature of its connections globally. Followers of Jesus of Nazareth were first called disciples since they were students of the Teacher (Rabbi) Jesus. When Jesus sent out his disciples, however, he deemed them apostles. Apostles were messengers sent to deliver the teachings of and to witness to the power of Jesus Christ. They did so in word and deed, inviting people to repent of their sin and be forgiven by the Triune God, while casting out evil spirits, healing, and performing other miracles as signs of God's power among them. We will start by looking at the apostolic mission since the Christian mission was carried initially by this small group of apostles. What we learn is that Christianity's orientation is inherently missionary; it is a sent faith that moves out from centers to peripheries.

The apostolic mission engaged with a wide variety of peoples and cultures, forcing the apostles to communicate the Christian faith in meaningful ways in different contexts. In the Christian encounter with others, apostles (and later, missionaries) translated the gospel into categories, languages, and meaning systems understood by local recipients. Apostles were talking about God in new ways. They were doing theology. Christian mission gave birth to theology, as messengers communicated in word and deed the gospel of Jesus Christ. This process gave rise to Christian plurality, a kind of diversity unparalleled in other religions.

The chapter provides snapshots of Christianity around the world to underscore the universal and particular themes of the faith. Christianity, interconnected globally, is "catholic" (universal). That is, Christianity consists of an organic fellowship of Christ-followers consisting not of disparate groups of believers existing independently of one another, but of numerous local assemblies bound by their shared unity in the life, death, and resurrection of Jesus Christ. Common fellowship binds Christians together, yet particular cultural traits of worship and theology are maintained.

Finally, the chapter ends with a discussion of the global shifts of Christianity and the numbers of Christians worldwide. What I argue here is that the numbers themselves, while important, communicate only a part of the story of Christianity around the globe. For instance, the number of Christians has shifted dramatically since the late twentieth century, where the majority of Christians now live in the Global South. This trend will probably continue, making Christianity increasingly non-Western. However, the economic, publishing, and educational power and influence still reside in the Global North. Numbers have shifted, but power and authority less so.

Chapter 3 focuses on the most popular book in the world when answering the question, Why is the Bible so important to Christians? The word "Bible," meaning "books," is a collection of books written over a period of 1,500 years. Remarkable is the fact that despite its multiple authors, the Bible's message of the Triune God who loves and forgives humanity despite their disobedience (i.e., sin) remains a consistent theme. The Bible is unique for many reasons, but most importantly it is a text whose authors were inspired by the Holy Spirit. As the early Protestant Reformers stated, the words of the Bible reveal the Word, Jesus Christ. What does the Bible say? How was it put together? These and other questions will be answered in this chapter as we explore why the Bible is a crucial part of the life of Christians.

One of the most fascinating topics, and one that is often taken for granted by Christians, is the translatability of the Bible; that is, the sacred text can be and ought to be translated into vernacular languages around the world. The translation of the Bible reflects the fact that the final destination of the Christian message is every language and ethnic group, without giving priority to any language or culture in particular. The Bible's message, read in local languages, has had a massive impact on the world. For instance, the translation of the Bible has led many nationalist movements to overthrow colonial powers, based in part on the Christian notion that all people bear the image of God (*imago Dei*) and therefore ought never to be subjected by others. Yet the Bible's impact is not limited to the corporate sphere, for countless individual lives have been transformed by its message.

Chapter 4, "What Is the Christian Church?" explores the church as the body of Jesus Christ in the world as he was in the world. The church, both one and many, consists at once of the universal body of believers ("the church") as well as numerous particular congregations in time and space ("churches"). The proliferation of churches has been a strength and weakness of the faith, for disagreements among Christians and denominations have splintered Christianity, regardless of the common elements affirmed by Christian orthodoxy. But the church remains the people of God, created by the Spirit of God for the purpose of being the sign and instrument of the Triune God's work in the world.

Sociologically, the church seems like other voluntary institutions since it consists of people who voluntarily gather together with a particular purpose. Yet the church is unique because it is considered the body of Christ, which means that the *being* of the church is particular, unlike any other institution. The church consists of all kinds of people: women, men, children, wealthy and poor, educated and uneducated, "Jew and gentile"—that is, anyone who has faith in Jesus Christ. As the assembly, the church exists as believers of the Triune God.

Furthermore, the church is active inside and outside its gathering. Inside, the church gathers to receive teaching, celebrate the sacraments, and enjoy fellowship. Outside, the church seeks to live out the gospel in word and deed in countless ways that address individual and corporate brokenness and injustice. The church is sent out to share the good news of the kingdom of God with others. As such, the church focuses both inwardly and outwardly, with a goal of extending an invitation to all people to receive forgiveness and peace with the Triune God.

Chapter 5, "How Do Christians Worship?" focuses on one of the most personal aspects of being Christian—the center of Christian life together—worship. All human beings worship, in the sense that they ascribe worth to people and things. What we worship as ultimate will profoundly shape our self-perceptions, ambitions, joys, and fears.

Christian worship entails more than giving the Triune God honor and respect, since it enables human beings to be reoriented to what matters most. Some worship is organized by a liturgy, the order of service that involves rituals of public celebrations that guide worship in a structured way. Other kinds of worship do not contain liturgy, such as when individuals praise God outside public worship. When one speaks of liturgy, though, one is usually referring to corporate worship within the church. Therefore, worship can be done both within and outside of the four walls of the church.

How does one make sense of the immense diversity of Christian worship, where some forms are exuberant, loud, and energetic, while others are quiet, contemplative, and meditative? Some worship services last twenty minutes, and others last all day. There is a church in East Asia that typically worships eight hours on Sunday but monthly worships for twenty-four hours nonstop. Some churches have tens of thousands of people at Sunday worship. These are prominent spaces, often the largest properties in the city. Yet others worship in small gatherings, such as in apartments or offices. Despite the size of the assembly, language, culture, or liturgy, there are common features of corporate Christian worship all over the world, including meeting weekly, public Bible reading, celebrating the Lord's Supper (i.e., Eucharist, Mass, Communion), singing, prayer, teaching and preaching, and offering. What makes each worshiping community different is, in part, the emphases that each assembly stresses on individual elements of worship, with some foregrounding one particular feature (e.g., the Lord's Supper) over others (e.g., singing). In addition, theological differences contribute to distinct worship styles.

Chapter 6, "Where Is Christianity Going?" looks at the possible and surprising changes afoot in Christianity. The past three decades have witnessed massive demographic shifts within Christianity. Where are signs of Christianity's future growth and decline? Despite the impossibility of predicting the future of Christianity with any precision, broad trends point to dramatic alterations to Christianity worldwide. Accompanying these demographic changes are questions that emerge from these settings. Answers to these questions will impact how Christianity is conceived and lived out. Why? Because of the inextricable connection between Christianity and culture.

When Christianity, which is always in culture, is adopted by a new culture and people, it is reconceived in ways that make sense in its new surroundings. New questions emerge from these new contexts that force Christians to articulate a response. For example, How does one contend against oppressive powers, both structural and spiritual? How does one live faithfully in areas of the world that prohibit Christian worship? How does one think about faith in terms of local ethical systems? How does one relate to Hindus, Buddhists, Muslims, secularists, and "nones"?

On the one hand, Christianity's future will continue to be marked by similar geographic and cultural shifts that have marked its history, with numerical ascension and recession in each region. The numbers of Christians will rise and fall across the globe. At the same time, Christianity will also be increasingly carried by digital media, having an ephemeral quality to it, replete with virtual churches pastored by Internet pastors, where face-to-face worship will be replaced by digitally mediated experiences. This is Internet Christianity, where one can be entirely anonymous and yet enjoy the benefits of teaching, worship, and sacraments in a shared virtual space.

Where is Christianity going? How will it be reinterpreted as it goes? Two topics will certainly shape the future of Christianity: social migration and the growth of a disembodied faith. The first will have dramatic effects on Christian theology—that is, how we talk about the Triune God. Social mobility changes the way people see God. When moving from their home regions to entirely new areas, migrants are forced to think of Christian faith in new ways. For example, What resources of Christian faith will help in this new surrounding? How do I relate to people different than me? Migration raises some of the most challenging issues for one's identity, and Christians have used their faith to provide wisdom in the midst of those changes. The second topic that will reshape the way we understand Christianity is the challenge of incarnational presence. With the burgeoning of virtual worship spaces comes the false substitution for being fully present in a face-to-face community. Internet Christianity will increasingly be a feature of the landscape of Christianity worldwide. What are the benefits and drawbacks of this new form of Christianity?

Chapter 7, "How Does Christianity Relate to Other Religions?," presents Christianity in the context of other religions. Here I compare elements of Christianity to features of other faith traditions in order to tease out similarities and differences among the religions, underscoring Christian uniqueness. Again, as we will discover, the context of Christianity is important, since there is no such thing as a pure Christianity—that is, one without context. How is Christianity understood in the multiscriptural context of Asia, where there are countless sacred texts from Hinduism, Buddhism, Sikhism, Islam, Taoism, and Confucianism? Likewise, there are numerous similarities of ideas, what some have called "notional similarities," between Christianity and the other world religions. One notional similarity is "God," also referred to as "Allah" by Muslims and "Brahman" by Hindus. Because a religion uses the same term when translated into English ("God"), does that imply that the notions are the same or only similar? The answer to this question makes a huge difference to how one understands religions comparatively.

Finally, given Christianity's global reach, we will want to explore some of the unique challenges it faces as it encounters other religions. Christianity affirms the centrality of history as the arena in which the Triune God has been revealed. For instance, Christians underscore the historicity of Jesus of Nazareth as a testimony to the veracity of Christian faith. But other religions (e.g., Hinduism, Buddhism) have absolutely no problem affirming that truth can be conveyed outside of history. Furthermore, what might other religions remind Christianity of that already resides within the Christian tradition but is no longer widely practiced, such as meditation?

Back to photography. Once when I was photographing a baseball game, a professional photographer told me not to capture just the powerful hit, ball on bat, but to turn around in the stands and take a photograph of the fans going crazy with excitement because of the home run. That makes a compelling image. We like to see that kind of emotion in photography. I hope you will see in this book a similar dynamic range of images: a view of Christianity that focuses on both the bat-on-ball realities of the faith (e.g., doctrines, beliefs) as well as its larger context (e.g., cultures) of the participants enjoying the thrill of the game.

# 1

# Who Are Christians?

Now those who had been scattered by the persecution that broke out when Stephen was killed traveled as far as Phoenicia, Cyprus and Antioch, spreading the word only among Jews. Some of them, however, men from Cyprus and Cyrene, went to Antioch and began to speak to Greeks also, telling them the good news about the Lord Jesus. The Lord's hand was with them, and a great number of people believed and turned to the Lord. . . .

Then Barnabas went to Tarsus to look for Saul, and when he found him, he brought him to Antioch. So for a whole year Barnabas and Saul met with the church and taught great numbers of people. The disciples were called Christians first at Antioch.

Acts 11:19–21, 25–26

My first experience with Christianity was as a member of St. Vartan Armenian Apostolic Church in Oakland, California, where I spent the first decade of my life. Despite having little appreciation for the rich liturgical life of Eastern Orthodoxy as a young boy, I knew something extraordinary was going on in worship as I heard the bells, saw the ornate altar, smelled the fragrant incense wafting through the sanctuary, and ate the bread and drank the wine

1

of the Eucharist. It was a total experience, each week rehearsing the grand narrative of Christian faith in 3D, invoking the names of past saints and current bishops. What I recall was overhearing a dialogue between the fancily dressed priest, situated near a raised altar in the front of the sanctuary, and the elevated choir, standing in the choir loft in the rear of the church. Priest and choir provided the heavenly discourse, and we, the congregation sitting in pews below, were privy to the retelling of the grand narrative of God's creation and redemption of the world.

After the service my sisters, cousins, and other congregants would gather in the fellowship hall and learn traditional Armenian dancing, enjoying culinary delicacies such as baklava or choereg. When I was about ten years old, our mother decided to take us out of the Armenian Church because, as she would say, "The Armenian Church is all about Armenian culture, not about the gospel. We will never hear the gospel here." So we changed churches. What was ironic, at least from my perspective, was that we left the Armenian Church to avoid "culture" but moved to the Swedish Covenant Church, a church rooted in the Lutheran Church of Sweden. Had we really left culture to embrace *just* the gospel? We left the Kazarians, Harotoonians, Ohanesians, and other Armenian families, and were adopted into a community of Larsons, Carlsons, and Johnsons. We exchanged baklava for Swedish meatballs. From one perspective, the change from Orthodoxy to Protestantism meant that we had become Christians—that is, believers in the good news of salvation in Christ. Some Christians believe that only Protestantism or Catholicism or Eastern Orthodoxy is Christian. Others see that Christianity itself is one, with many streams identified as Roman Catholic, Eastern Orthodox, and Protestant. From that perspective, we never left Christianity.

## Two Marks of Being Christian

When you hear the word "Christian," what images come to mind? Mother Teresa or Martin Luther King Jr.? Narrow-minded people who follow a set of moralistic beliefs and practices? European Cathedrals? Baptist, Catholic, or Pentecostal? Republican or Democrat?

Everyone has an opinion about Christianity. But what does it mean to be Christian?

In this chapter I answer the question, Who are Christians? by discussing "Christian" as both noun and modifier. Most generally, the term "Christian" describes a person (noun) who trusts Jesus and affirms the Triune God as described in the Bible, and it also describes a change in direction (modifier) that creates new meaning and gives new direction to all things.[1] To engage the question, What is Christianity? this chapter considers the following six topics: (1) what early Christians said about themselves, (2) how they became a new moral community, (3) how they understood conversion to Christianity, (4) how Christianity engaged with culture, (5) the concept of orthodoxy, and, finally, (6) how the "rules of faith" continue to guide Christians around the world. Before I launch into these subjects, I need to introduce two broad themes about being Christian.

There are two primary marks of being a Christian, with the first being foundational for the second. The first mark centers on the creation of something new, which is often called regeneration. Regeneration is used to describe a process of restoration and growth that brings new life and strength, particularly in the context of disturbance. Being Christian means having received something particular, the gospel of Jesus Christ, whereby God gives new life from a previous state of eternal death and separation from God. There's a lot here to unpack: "the gospel," "Jesus Christ," "God," are weighty terms that are debated both within and outside of Christian circles. These terms will be discussed throughout this book since they are central to being Christian. The Bible too becomes an essential part of our conversation, for it is from the Bible that we learn that the state of humanity is seriously flawed and yet God still loves human beings. The Bible describes humanity as being deeply sinful (Rom. 3:23; Gal. 3:22), a condition that separates humanity from God, who deeply loves us regardless (John 3:16; Rom. 5:8).

Since God is divine, holy, perfect, all-powerful, and all-knowing, human beings cannot stand before God without being conspicuously

---

1. "Triune God" refers to the affirmation of God the Father, God the Son, and God the Holy Spirit as a unity—a triunity or Trinity.

guilty of their imperfection—a condition that the Bible refers to as "sin." An illustration will suffice: If we attend a formal wedding but wear clothes with large stains, we feel out of place, even ashamed. Much more so when humans recognize their stained condition before the Holy God. Because of God's love for creation, God sent Jesus Christ, the incarnation of God, to pay the penalty for our sin—the stain—and satisfy God's wrath by dying on the cross in our place, thus enabling a relationship with God to be restored (Gal. 4:4–7; 1 Tim. 2:4–6).

Christians place their faith in the work that Christ did on the cross to enable a relationship with the living God. Therefore, the first and most important mark of being a Christian is that we must first ask God to forgive us of our sins and then be committed to follow Christ. Grace—the unmerited favor of God—is what effects the change in the human relationship with God, since there is nothing human beings can do to gain God's forgiveness by their own efforts. When we ask God for forgiveness for the sin in our life and have faith in what Christ did on the cross by shedding his blood, we are Christians. People all around the world have experienced this forgiveness and regeneration.

A second mark of being a Christian entails the reception of gifts from God for the betterment of the church, society, and the natural world. While there are forms of Christianity that entail retreating from the common life of society, Christianity itself is not a movement of withdrawal. Rather than being isolationist, being Christian propels one into the world to make all things better. The Bible tells of spiritual gifts given by the Holy Spirit to Christians in order to strengthen the church and to benefit the world. Some of these include apostles, healing, service, mercy, teaching, wisdom, and exhortation (Rom. 12:3–8; 1 Cor. 12:7–11; Eph. 4:11–12). The purpose of these gifts is to serve and glorify God and uplift others. Spiritual gifts are often distinguished from natural talents that enable us to do physical abilities, such as music, art, or carpentry. Christians employ their gifts and talents toward purposeful living so that Christians might "do good works, which God prepared in advance for us to do" (Eph. 2:10). This kind of living has contributed to the shaping of societies and cultures around the world, as Christians often were the first to establish centers of education and healthcare as an expression of Christian commitment to the betterment of others. Some of the greatest universities and hospitals in the world were started by Christians living out their Christian faith to help others.

These two primary marks of being Christian, being oriented toward the Triune God and being oriented toward our fellow human beings and the natural world, are sometimes referred to as "orthodoxy" and "orthopraxy," where orthodoxy refers to right belief (faith) and orthopraxy to right practice (works, actions). Together, orthodoxy and orthopraxy give us a fairly broad way to see being Christian as an orientation that is at once vertical, since it enables a relationship with the Triune God, and horizontal, since it cannot exist without its expression toward others. Becoming Christian is so profound that the Bible describes the process as being "born again," "made alive," and becoming "saints" and "children of God" (e.g., John 1:12; Rom. 8:14; Gal. 3:26; Eph. 2:5; 1 John 3:1).

Being Christian does not entail being a part of a particular political party, economic system, culture, race, or ethnicity. Christianity is at once above these categories since all Christians are united regardless of these identifications and are deeply engaged in these particular features of individual and social life.

In the first few centuries of Christianity, a community of Christians would gather around a particular teacher, paralleling the teacher-disciple relationship popular in that day. While there were similarities with other communities, much in the way of Christian thinking and acting contrasted starkly with the religious and moral life propounded in the Greco-Roman world. That Christians too had a school of thought was reflected in Justin Martyr's comment that Christianity was "the true philosophy" when compared to other schools of antiquity. Paul and other early church leaders of his circle, like other moral teachers of their day, carried on teaching and discipling activities. New believers were instructed in the beliefs and norms and admonished where needed, similar to the way people were instructed and admonished by the Hellenistic moral discourses of the first century.

One of the stark differences within the Christian community compared to other groups of the day was that the Christian community had a reputation for charitable activities, seeking to alleviate suffering and sharing their substances: "faith by itself, if it is not accompanied by action, is dead" (James 2:17). Rodney Stark notes that in contrast to Christian charity, "In the pagan world, and especially among the philosophers, mercy was regarded as a character defeat and pity as a pathological emotion: because mercy involves providing *unearned* help or relief, it is contrary to justice."[2] Early Christians, by comparison, were made new by being filled with the Holy Spirit (Acts 2:4; Eph. 5:18) and sought to extend mercy to others even when it was not reciprocal. The Bible says that the fruit of the Spirit is love, joy, peace, patience, kindness, goodness, faithfulness, gentleness, and self-control, against which there is no law (Gal. 5:22–23). In the midst of epidemics and pestilence, when pagans rejected the diseased, throwing them into the roads before they were dead, Christians actively showed compassion and saved large numbers of lives.[3]

The second-century apologetic document Epistle to Diognetus gives us insight into how early Christians were seen by their contemporaries.

> Christians are not distinguished from the rest of mankind by either country, speech, or customs; the fact is, they nowhere settle in cities of their own; they use no peculiar language; they cultivate no eccentric mode of life. . . . Yet while they dwell in both Greek and non-Greek cities, as each one's lot was cast, and conform to the customs of the country in dress, food, and mode of life in general, the whole tenor of their way of living stamps it as worthy of admiration and admittedly extraordinary. They reside in their respective countries, but only as aliens. They take part in everything as citizens and put up with everything as foreigners. Every foreign land is their home, and every home a foreign land.[4]

Christians were marked by faith, hope, and love (1 Cor. 13:13; Col. 1:5; 1 Thess. 1:3; 5:8), which distinguished them from their contemporaries. The Epistle to Diognetus notes that Christians followed the

2. Rodney Stark, *The Triumph of Christianity: How the Jesus Movement Became the World's Largest Religion* (New York: HarperOne, 2011), 112.
3. Stark, *Triumph of Christianity*, 115–17.
4. The entire statement can be found in the Epistle to Diognetus 5.1–5, in Johannes Quasten et al., eds., *Ancient Christian Writers: The Works of the Fathers in Translation* (New York: Newman, 1946), 6:138–39.

customs and traditions of their contemporaries regarding food and clothing, yet they dwelled in their communities as sojourners. Christians shared all things with one another. They repaid insults with honor, yet those who hated them were unable to assign any reason for their hatred.

Paul, to whom many New Testament books are attributed, tells the Thessalonians, "Encourage one another and build each other up, just as in fact you are doing" (1 Thess. 5:11). Christians were not to be separatists, isolated from the wider society. Paul, for instance, admonished fellow believers to concentrate on manual labor and self-sufficiency, illustrating that Christians were to be active in social and economic life. Paul was a tentmaker who supported himself as he was sent by God to share the gospel with gentiles.

Women too made up a large part of the Christian movement because they were attracted to Christianity's egalitarian spirit, at least in comparison to other ancient groups, such as Jewish and Hellenistic ones, which did not see women as equal to men. Indeed, throughout the New Testament there is evidence of women in church leadership (e.g., Rom. 16:1–2), as deacons, for instance. Many exceeded the roles of their Jewish and pagan women peers.

## What Did Early Christians Say about Themselves?

How did these early followers of Jesus understand themselves? First-century Christians consisted mostly of Jews who recognized Jesus as the Messiah. The first recorded usage of the term "Christian" is found in the New Testament. The term meant "follower of Christ": "The disciples were called Christians first at Antioch" (Acts 11:26). Within a century the Christian community had grown to include most ethnic groups in the Roman Empire, and their language was primarily Greek.

If we overheard what the first Christians called themselves as they were discovering their new identity, we would hear expressions such as "the churches of God," "the holy ones," "children of God," "slaves of Christ," "brothers and sisters," "those for whom Christ died."[5]

---

5. Wayne A. Meeks, *The Moral World of the First Christians* (Philadelphia: Westminster, 1986), 12.

Early Christians saw themselves as part of a new moral and spiritual community, a new humanity so grandly reconfigured that Paul writes, "Live lives worthy of God, who calls you" (1 Thess. 2:12). To be Christian was to be a part of a community marked by a certain character that was "expected to affect some of the most fundamental relationships, values, perceptions of reality, and even structures of the self."[6] To be Christian was not to join a particular culture, Jewish or gentile, but rather to be part of a movement referred to as the Jesus sect or the Way, a new beginning for all of creation.

Kinship language distinguished the vocabulary of early Christians from other contemporary social groupings, for they were called "brothers and sisters," "children of God," referring to one another as "beloved," no longer enemies but a new family of God (1 Thess. 1:4–6). The biblical account notes that Christians sought to please and serve God, who loved them enough to make each one "an heir, through God" (Gal. 4:7 NRSV).

Nothing like this existed in the Greco-Roman world since other movements were less inclusive and more socially stratified. All Christians were heirs, children of God. This fresh movement entailed a socialization that would even set biological family members against one another: "For I [Jesus] have come to set a man against his father, and a daughter against her mother, and a daughter-in-law against her mother-in-law" (Matt. 10:35 NRSV).[7] As reconfigured social boundaries were erected, while others were torn down, there emerged a new sociology of difference based on faith in Christ rather than blood or ethnicity. Followers of the Triune God (i.e., Father, Son, and Holy Spirit) did not consist of one ethnicity or race but rather were a new nation, a "chosen people" (1 Pet. 2:9).

## A New Moral Family and a New Loyalty

An important way to understand "Christian" as a chosen people is to consider the term as an adjective, a description of an orientation

6. Meeks, *Moral World of the First Christians*, 13.
7. See also Mark 3:31–35; Luke 14:26.

that sets it apart from other ways of living. "Christian" modifies life. Early Christians not only considered themselves as a new family; they also saw themselves as a new moral community that was distinct from the surrounding cultures. The first Christians met in house churches, where they formed ethical communities that followed moral guide-lines, not unlike some lists of the duties of members of households found in the writings of the Greek moralists of the time. Such house lists appeared in ancient Greek, Jewish, and Christian writings, offer-ing instruction about a wide range of topics, such as how to behave toward God, the state, marriage partners, and children.[8] These moral guidelines were not free from conflict with surrounding communi-ties. In fact, significant disruption plagued the lives of converts to Christianity, even to the point of facing death (Acts 7:54–60), as they embraced a faith that reoriented their lives around the Triune God rather than Greco-Roman deities or other religions.

Joining these house churches, which were guided by house duties, created tension between the Christian community and prevailing cul-ture and its leaders. But these gatherings helped to erect boundaries based on faith in Christ alone rather than shared culture or ethnicity. What is unique about the New Testament moral exhortations is that they are not simply "Christianized" versions of previous or contem-poraneous moral admonitions. Rather, they give us insight into how the inner life of a Christian community, including the relationships among its members, was viewed in relationship to the wider society that was distrustful of it.[9]

With the emergence of the Christian community in the Greco-Roman world, two robustly religious cultures came into conflict. Loyalty to the Triune God conflicted with loyalty to the emperor, who was to be worshiped. This led to horrendous persecution of Christian communities since allegiance of these Christian groups to one another supplanted all other loyalties. According to the Christian community, the gods of the Greco-Roman world, which controlled every aspect of living, were powerless in relationship to Jesus Christ,

8. See Abraham J. Malherbe, *Social Aspects of Early Christianity* (Philadelphia: Fortress, 1983), 51.
9. Malherbe, *Social Aspects of Early Christianity*, 53.

God incarnate. Christian fidelity to household members (the house church) surpassed allegiance to the republic, as Christians believed themselves to have "been called to a higher quality of their life than could be expected of their society."[10] Such opposition to gods and emperor was met with the onslaught of terrible violence against the Christian community. Early sources state that Christians were convicted of *odium humani generis* ("hatred of the human race"). The Roman historian Tacitus (58–120 CE), reflecting on the treatment of Christians under the emperor Nero (37–68 CE), offers the following account of the horrendous persecution of Christians:

> [Nero] blamed and savagely punished people popularly hated for their crimes and called Christians. . . . A sport was made of their execution. Some, sewn in the skins of animals, were torn apart by dogs. Others were crucified or burned, and others, as darkness drew on, were used as torches. Nero devoted his gardens to the spectacle, provided a circus, and himself, in the costume of a charioteer, rode around among the crowd, until compassion began to arise for the victims, who though deserving of the severest penalties, were actually suffering not for the public good but to glut the cruelty of one man.[11]

The Letter of 1 Peter was written to a community undergoing various forms of persecution and is replete with practical encouragement to new believers. "Live such good lives among the pagans that, though they accuse you of doing wrong, they may see your good deeds and glorify God on the day he visits us" (1 Pet. 2:12); "Do not repay evil with evil or insult with insult. On the contrary, repay evil with blessing, because to this you were called so that you may inherit a blessing" (3:9). Early believers were derided (2:12), insulted (3:9), made to suffer (3:14), and abused (4:4). Their conflict with authorities was real and so was their fervent commitment to one another. These Christian communities were given instruction on how to relate to governmental authorities (2:13–17), spouses—wives to husbands (3:1–6) and husbands to wives (3:7)—and one another (3:8–9).

10. Malherbe, *Social Aspects of Early Christianity*, 69.
11. Roland H. Bainton, *Christendom: A Short History of Christianity and Its Impact on Western Civilization*, 2 vols. (New York: Harper & Row, 1966), 1:51.

While Christian communities were "foreigners and exiles" and were called on to abstain from sinful desires that waged against the soul (1 Pet. 2:11), they constituted a new family of believers (2:17) and "a responsible part of society and represent a quality of life that is intelligible enough to outsiders to function as a missionary witness and defense."[12] In the words of the Gospel of John, "They are not of the world, even as I [Jesus Christ] am not of it" (17:16), yet they are *in* the world for the purpose of being a sign and instrument of the kingdom of God. Despite being persecuted, with joyous anticipation the early Christian community awaited the return of the resurrected Christ.

## Convert and Proselyte Revisited

Early Christians were not born Christian. They *became* Christian. Becoming Christian required that they understood their culture in the light of the gospel. Yet that was not an easy task. Famously, as gentiles began to convert from paganism to Christianity, a dispute arose over whether gentiles had to adopt Jewish traditions, particularly male circumcision, if they wanted to become followers of the Messiah, whom Christians recognized as Jesus Christ. During the Jerusalem Council (Acts 15:1–35), the heated debate (cf. Gal. 2:11–14) ended with the affirmation that all people and all cultures can follow the Messiah without the requirement to adopt Jewish practices (although the Council did insist that gentile believers adhere to certain dietary restrictions and avoid sexual immorality).

Earlier, in response to a vision from God, Peter said, "I now realize how true it is that God does not show favoritism but accepts from every nation the one who fears him and does what is right" (Acts 10:34–35). This "gentile breakthrough" showed that Christianity promotes cultural pluralism in the light of the Triune God; that is, there are countless ways that Christianity can be and ought to be communicated through cultures. In the words of Calvin Shenk, "The

12. Bainton, *Christendom*, 1:53. See also Stanley Hauerwas and William H. Willimon, *Resident Aliens: Life in the Christian Colony* (Nashville: Abingdon, 1989).

Gentile breakthrough had cast a shadow over any claims for Jewish cultural absolutism."[13] Yet the task of negotiating the relationship between gospel and culture would not be an easy one.

Two terms have been used to illustrate two basic ways that the gospel relates to culture: "proselyte" and "convert." According to the proselyte model, someone from outside the Christian fold is welcomed in but must adopt the fold's culture, practices, and ways of knowing.[14] For instance, rather than interpreting Christian faith through one's own culture, a proselyte accepts the practices of other Christians as most meaningful. When some Christians initially argued that gentiles who wanted to follow the Messiah (Jesus Christ) were to be circumcised, they were advocating for a proselyte model. The proselyte model contrasts with the convert model.

A convert takes what is already there in a given location—for instance, the system of symbols, philosophies, life situation—and turns those to Christ. The revelation of Christ gives those symbols new meaning, completes them, and not only makes them new but also transforms them into channels of revelation. Symbols, then, are reconfigured to convey and be conduits of God's self-disclosure. Two of the most common biblical illustrations of conversion come to mind.

The first involves the importance of lambs in Hebrew culture and religious life. The ritual of lamb sacrifice, so essential to Hebrew tradition, is completed by Christ's death and resurrection. Upon seeing Jesus, John the Baptizer exclaimed, "Look, the Lamb of God, who takes away the sin of the world!" (John 1:29), since Jesus would satisfy the wrath of God, completing the ritual to which the lamb sacrifice only pointed. The revelation of Jesus Christ satisfied the earlier longing, which the ritual could only anticipate.

A second biblical example is the Gospel of John's use of the Greek term *logos*, meaning "Word," "Divine Reason," "Ground"—that which orders the cosmos and gives it meaning. Logos was found in Greek, Indian, Egyptian, and Persian philosophical and theological

13. Calvin E. Shenk, *Who Do You Say That I Am? Christians Encounter Other Religions* (1997; repr., Eugene, OR: Wipf & Stock, 2006), 186.

14. Andrew F. Walls, "Converts or Proselytes? The Crisis over Conversion in the Early Church," *International Bulletin of Missionary Research* 28, no. 1 (2004): 5.

systems. The Gospel of John identifies Jesus Christ as "the Word" (Logos) made flesh (John 1:1; 1 John 1:1). John used the term to communicate to his Hellenistic readers in a strikingly potent way that Jesus Christ was the historical flesh-and-blood embodiment of Logos. The Logos is a person, Jesus Christ, who is God. What was an impersonal force in Greek philosophy becomes personified in Jesus Christ in the New Testament. Furthermore, it was the seed of reason (*logos spermatikos*) in Jesus Christ "which enabled pagan thinkers like Socrates to see dimly what came to be clearly seen through the revelation of the Logos in the person of Jesus."[15] Indeed, the Christ event changed all of history.

Employed by the biblical writers, "Lamb" and "Logos" are not only communicative devices to convey the message of Jesus Christ; they also suggest that older symbols (e.g., lambs, Logos) are not eradicated by the Christian revelation. Rather, symbols are made complete, reaching their intended maturity only hinted at in their original state, as the revelation of Christ is brought to bear on them. Mircea Eliade suggested the same, in this case in regard to water as a symbol, when he discussed the uniqueness of the Christian revelation in his book *The Sacred and the Profane*: "The revelation brought by the [Christian] faith did not destroy pre-Christian meanings of symbols; it simply added a new value to them. . . . For the believer this new meaning eclipsed all the others; it *alone* valorized the symbol, transfigured it into revelation. . . . It could even be said that the aquatic symbol *awaited* the fulfillment of its deepest meaning through the new values contributed by Christianity."[16] When fulfilled by Christ, symbols become channels of the revelation of the Triune God.

If you are uncomfortable with the term "symbol" because it sounds too abstract and disconnected from daily life, keep in mind that I am using the term to connote anything in our daily life that points to something invisible, usually greater than itself. For example, when we are driving, a "stop sign" means more than a red sign with the

15. Jaroslav Pelikan, *The Christian Tradition: A History of the Development of Doctrine*, vol. 1, *Emergence of the Catholic Tradition (100–600)* (Chicago: University of Chicago Press, 1971), 32.

16. Mircea Eliade, *The Sacred and the Profane: The Nature of Religion*, trans. Willard R. Trask (New York: Harcourt, Brace, 1959), 137.

word "stop" emblazoned on it. Symbols, as actions (e.g., bowing), words (e.g., "good morning"), and objects (e.g., water), are pointers. When we see two people shaking hands, we interpret that as a greeting or as an agreement. In this sense, symbols reflect what is important to our corporate lives, since they convey knowledge of our entire personal, social, cultural, and religious inheritance. This view is broad enough to entail systems of philosophy and culture as well as narrow enough to apply to individuals and existential concerns; the revelation of Christ covers all things.

There are huge implications to whether we understand "Christian" to be something imported from outside our personal and corporate reality (proselyte) instead of emerging primarily from within our own context (conversion). Regarding the proselyte/convert model, Andrew Walls suggests, "The essence of the [proselytizing] tendency is the insistence on imposing our own religious culture, our own Torah and circumcision. Christian conversion as demonstrated in the New Testament is not about substituting something new for something old—that is to move back to the proselyte model, which the apostolic church could have adopted but decided to abandon."[17] The majority of early Christians lived in urban areas throughout the Roman Empire, where discrete categories of local (convert) and nonlocal (proselyte) could not be sustained as separate classifications since there was much sharing among a large variety of peoples and cultures.

Dual directionality emerged when one became a Christian. One direction to which the new faith pointed was to a deepened understanding of one's own culture: Logos and lamb were understood differently in the light of the revelation of Christ.[18] Christ freed both Jews and Greeks, being the sacrificial Lamb to the former and the incarnation of the Logos for the latter. Ethnicity was not eliminated. It was deepened. The other direction to which faith pointed was to a greater sense of shared humanity, based primarily on the recognition of the presence of the image of God (*imago Dei*) in all persons.

17. Walls, "Converts or Proselytes?," 6.
18. See, Charles E. Farhadian, "Beyond Lambs and Logos: Christianity, Cultures, and Worship Worldwide," in *Christian Worship Worldwide: Expanding Horizons, Deepening Practices*, ed. Charles E. Farhadian (Grand Rapids: Eerdmans, 2007), 1–24.

## Nothing Is Christian ... at the Start

Of course, "Christian" refers to content, knowledge, and experience. But perhaps it is more fruitful to understand the term as referring to direction more than content. In its adjectival form, "Christian" describes a person, group, or idea that has been transformed by the Christian revelation. "Christian Japanese" describes the orientation of one or more Japanese. "Christian" does not eliminate "Japanese"; it deepens it. Likewise, "Christian philosophy" describes an orientation of metaphysics, epistemology, and ethics.

People and ideas have the potential to be Christian, but nothing is inherently Christian, at the start. Everything that we equate with being Christian existed prior to the rise of Christianity. With the coming of Jesus Christ, everything changed. Referring to the changes brought by the revelation of Jesus Christ, Lesslie Newbigin wrote, "Something happened that alters the total human situation."[19] What changes transpired? The old was made new, transformed to become a conduit of new life for believers. Christians did not create new ideas out of nothing. Yet the gospel that was communicated by the apostle Paul and others was unique, a peculiar message not of human origin but received by the revelation of Jesus Christ (Gal. 1:11–12). And that revelation changed everything.

For instance, prior to the early third century there is no evidence of Christian art. Clement of Alexandria (150–215 CE) suggested that a Christian who wanted to have a ring that expressed Christian faith should purchase a ring whose figures could be given a Christian meaning. Furthermore, Clement's view applies to other objects, the structure of letter writing, and rhetoric as well. Robert Louis Wilken explains,

> As yet there were no Christian artists or craftsmen who designed objects with distinctive Christian images. So Clement recommends that Christians buy rings that were in common use and readily available in workshops in the markets of the city. Though they may be stamped with symbols that bear one meaning to the maker and to most buyers,

19. Lesslie Newbigin, *Foolishness to the Greeks: The Gospel and Western Culture* (Grand Rapids: Eerdmans, 1986), 3.

some of the engravings could be given a Christian sense. A dove could
be taken to symbolize the Christian virtue of gentleness and peace-
fulness; a fish could be a symbol of Christ because the letters of the
Greek word for fish (*ixthus*) could be taken to spell the first letters of
the words JESUS CHRIST SON OF GOD SAVIOR; a ship could signify the
Church carrying the faithful over the turbulent waters of life; a young
man with a lyre could depict David singing the psalms; and an anchor
could be a symbol of hope (Heb. 6:18–19).[20]

Christians adopted what was already in a specific location and re-
inscribed those items (e.g., oil lamp, bowl, pitcher) with Christian
meaning. Nothing was Christian in the beginning. They were *made*
Christian by their new orientation in the light of the revelation of
Jesus Christ. Paul, for instance, followed a common letter-writing
strategy and structure when composing his epistles, which were
typical of his first-century contemporaries. Paul inherited that letter-
writing strategy, but he redirected it to convey the Christian message.
Here are some other examples of concepts that were adopted and
transformed by the revelation of Christ and now are considered essential to Christianity.

First, *ekklēsia* ("church"), the community of God's people, appears in the New Testament. Yet this Greek term predated Christianity. In its original usage, *ekklēsia* meant a voluntary organization
of freed male Roman citizens.[21] The term referred to a gathering,
congregation, assembly, and in classical Greek referred almost exclusively to a political gathering. Paul redefined *ekklēsia* in the light
of the revelation of Christ to be an assembly of the people of God,
not just a mere civic grouping.

Second, *kyrios* ("lord") is taken from *kyrios* Serapis (a Greco-
Roman deity) or *kyrios* Adonis, and thus predates Christianity. In
classical Greek *kyrios* meant "lord of the house" or simply "Lord,"
and the term was used in Hellenistic literature to describe gods and
goddesses. Roman emperors were often called *kyrios*, connecting

20. Robert Louis Wilken, *The First Thousand Years: A Global History of Christianity* (New Haven: Yale University Press, 2012), 49.
21. See, e.g., Wayne A. Meeks, *The First Urban Christians: The Social World of
the Apostle Paul* (New Haven: Yale University Press), 108.

them to a deity. *Kyrios* is also used in nonreligious contexts for "master." The biblical writers, however, applied *kyrios* to Jesus Christ, using it 740 times in the New Testament to refer to Jesus as the believers' Lord and Master who would one day judge them with a power beyond that of Roman emperors and secular masters. Indeed, Lord Jesus is "the Lord of both the dead and the living" (Rom. 14:9), and his return marks "the day of the Lord" (1 Thess. 5:2). Christians did not invent the term *kyrios*; they adopted it from Greco-Roman religion and redirected it.

Third, the notion of baptism predates Christianity as an Old Testament and Jewish initiatory ritual. In fact, the ritual use of water appears in many ancient Near Eastern religions as well as most religions worldwide and is used for purification purposes. Baptism is not Christian in origin. In first-century Judaism, God instructs Jews to cleanse themselves from ritual impurities through washing, a fulfillment of the legal requirements of ritual purity (Lev. 15:11–14). Full-body immersion, known as *tevilah* in Hebrew, involved ritual bathing in order to remove specifically defined uncleanliness prior to engaging in a particular type of activity, such as worship. The Gospel of Matthew records the encounter between Jesus and John the Baptizer and gives us insight on a fresh view of baptism: "Then Jesus came from Galilee to the Jordan to be baptized by John. But John tried to deter him, saying, 'I need to be baptized by you, and do you come to me?' Jesus replied, 'Let it be so now; it is proper for us to do this to *fulfill all righteousness.*' Then John consented" (Matt. 3:13–15). Jesus Christ fulfills all righteousness; he establishes peace over a creation that was marked by the chaos of sin. Compared to earlier forms, Jesus's baptism is unique in that he emerges victorious from the waters to become the head of a new community.

At the end of the second century, Tertullian wrote that it mattered that one be baptized, but it did not matter whether one was baptized in the "sea or pond, river or spring, lake or river bed."[22] Wilken notes that in the early church there was "no Christianity without a bath,

22. Ernest Evans, *Tertullian's Treatise on the Incarnation: The Text with an Introduction, Translation and Commentary* (1956; repr., Eugene, OR: Wipf & Stock, 2016), 139.

without passing through the waters of baptism."[23] While the current practice of baptism varies widely in the Christian church, and is a source of some debate, Jesus commanded his disciples to "make disciples . . . , baptizing them in the name of the Father and of the Son and of the Holy Spirit" (Matt. 28:19). Baptism, whether by immersion or sprinkling, was a concept embraced and practiced by Christians to tell the story of Jesus overcoming death and providing new life.

Fourth, the idea of "redemption" precedes Christianity. The motif of redemption is prominent throughout the New Testament. Yet New Testament authors inherited the concept from Greco-Roman and Jewish literature. Classical Greek texts used the term *apolytrōsis* ("redemption") to refer to the ransom payment given to release a slave, a condemned criminal, or a captive of war. What is powerful about the New Testament use of the term is that it was applied to Jesus (Rom. 3:24; 1 Cor. 1:30; Eph. 1:7; Col. 1:13–14), who himself is the "ransom" (*lytron*) for many (Matt. 20:28; Mark 10:45). Redemption did not mean freedom from relationships but incorporation into a new family. The Christian perspective, then, adopted and yet reconfigured the contemporary idea that captives and others sentenced to death can regain their life if someone purchases that life back with a ransom (Col. 1:13–14). Rather than a monetary notion of payment that remained outside of the redeemer, Jesus's blood paid the ransom (Eph. 1:7). The result was a new life no longer bound by sin (Gal. 5:1). Through redemption, all people are adopted as children of God into a new family based on faith in Jesus Christ.

Fifth, *diakonos* ("deacon") was common in secular Greek literature in the first century to refer to one whose function involved waiting on tables, one who serves.[24] *Diakonos* is used repeatedly throughout the New Testament in this sense.[25] However, biblical writers present *diakonos* to refer to ministers who serve God or Christ.[26] Paul formalizes the term to refer to a specific office of deacon (Phil. 1:1; 1 Tim. 3:8–12).

---

23. Robert Louis Wilken, *The Spirit of Early Christian Thought: Seeking the Face of God* (New Haven: Yale University Press, 2003), 36.
24. See Meeks, *First Urban Christians*, 79.
25. See, e.g., Matt. 20:26; 23:11; Mark 9:35; 10:43; John 2:9.
26. See, e.g., Rom. 13:4; Eph. 6:21; Col. 1:7; 1 Tim. 4:6.

The major concepts that gave shape to being Christian were adopted and transformed from the local contexts around the Roman Empire. Consequently, nothing is Christian at the start: terms that we associate with Christianity are redeemed from prior usage. This dynamic use of culture illustrates that Christianity employs culture as a vehicle to convey the good news, while transforming, by its redirection and fulfillment in Christ, the very elements of culture used to communicate the faith.

## The Parameters of Orthodoxy

If a Christian is one who has been converted to Christ, then what sets of beliefs guide Christian thinking and action? It is one thing to recognize that conversion entails coming to Christ through one's own culture, but are there universal themes that tie all Christians worldwide together? Is there a framework through which all these diverse expressions of Christian faith are lived out rightly? In other words, what are the shared beliefs of all Christians around the world? The diversity of Christianity around the world is set within the common themes laid out by the early church council meetings that defined the parameters of Christian orthodoxy. These common themes illustrate that "Christianity" is a noun, for it entails concrete beliefs that shape Christians worldwide.

At early ecumenical church council meetings, beginning in the early fourth century with the Council of Nicaea, the parameters of Christian "right belief" (orthodoxy) were established. These boundaries were broad, yet clearly stated. Let me offer a sports analogy to illustrate my point. Recognizing Christian orthodoxy is similar to recognizing a particular sport. Were we to visit Havana, Cuba, and watch a group of young people kicking a ball made of tape and cloth through a space whose boundaries are marked by two empty bottles placed on the ground a few feet from each other, we would be correct to assume that what we were watching was soccer, or as they would call it, fútbol. If there were no opposing sides, no goals into which to kick the ball, or no ball, that game would not be soccer. It might be something else, but not soccer. Likewise, an individual or social grouping that did not affirm Christian orthodoxy as established 1,500 years ago would not be Christian.

How were the boundaries of Christianity established? During the patristic period, the first five hundred years of Christianity, a consensus was reached at these ecumenical church councils about the parameters of Christian orthodoxy, which unified the Christian movement starting in the Roman Empire.[27] These historic debates consolidated Christian orthodoxy that became the foundation on which Christian belief and practice would be based from that time onward. All orthodox Christian churches trace themselves back to the decisions of these early ecumenical councils. Individuals and churches that live within and affirm the parameters of orthodoxy are considered Christian.

Two of the most salient affirmations agreed upon during these early ecumenical church council meetings were that (1) Jesus Christ is fully human and fully divine; Jesus was not created, not even the first of creation, but is God, of the exact same substance of God, a member of the triunity of the Godhead; and that (2) the Godhead consists of three persons and one essence; that is, the Triune God is one, existing as three persons: Father, Son, and Holy Spirit.

## Rule of Faith

Another important element that gives shape to being Christian is the Christian creeds. The creeds are statements of the shared beliefs of the Christian community that crystallize the decisions of the ecumenical church council meetings. The vast majority of Christians affirm historic creeds—that is, statements of Christian faith—the most widely accepted being the Apostles' Creed and the Nicene Creed. These statements of belief formed touchstones of Christian faith. It is important to recognize that creeds are based on the Bible, rather than vice versa, since the authority of the creeds is secondary to that of Scripture. Christian creeds were established in the

27. "Ecumenical" means the whole household of God. At these meetings, representatives from the church around the Roman Empire met to discuss and decide the basic affirmations of Christianity.

midst of theological disputes, some of which produced schisms in the Christian movement. For instance, Gnosticism, an amorphous group of schools of thought that flourished in the first and second centuries CE, claimed that salvation could be gained through secret knowledge (*gnōsis*) via mystical awareness based on direct experience of the Divine. The Gnostics argued that Christ was pure spirit whose body was only an apparition, a phantom. Gnosticism provided a formidable challenge to Christian orthodoxy, and early church leaders confronted those threats directly.[28]

The use of the creeds by early church leaders reflects a variety of interpretations. Jaroslav Pelikan notes that the creedal phrases in the writings of Irenaeus, Tertullian, and Hippolytus show great variation, adapted by these writers to suit their own purposes. Church leaders did, however, agree on common themes, referred to as a "rule of faith" or "rule of truth." According to Pelikan, "Two elements remain constant through the citations, and one or both of them may safely be said to have formed the outline of most creeds: Father, Son, and Holy Spirit; the life, death, and resurrection of Jesus Christ. These were, according to Origen, 'the particular points clearly delivered in the teaching of the apostles'; apostolic continuity, he argued, did not preclude discussion of other issues, but this central content was not negotiable."[29]

Early church leaders, such as Irenaeus (ca. 130–202 CE) and Tertullian (ca. 155–240 CE), spoke of the faith that the church had derived from Jesus's disciples and the apostles. According to one early tradition, after Pentecost (Acts 2:1–31), when the Holy Spirit descended on Christ's apostles and others gathered in Jerusalem and enabled them to speak in many languages in order to share the gospel to a variety of ethnic groups, the apostles gathered to draft the Apostles' Creed, "so that they might not find themselves, widely dispersed as they would be, delivering different messages."[30] This decision guaranteed doctrinal unity for apostolic continuity.

28. See, e.g., John 1:14; 1 Cor. 1:18–31; 15:53–54; Col. 2:8, 16–17; 1 Tim. 1:4; 6:20; 1 John 1:1–2; 2:22; 4:2–3.
29. Pelikan, *Emergence of the Catholic Tradition*, 117.
30. Rufinus, *Commentarius in symbolum apostolorum* 2, quoted in Pelikan, *Emergence of the Catholic Tradition*, 117.

## The Apostles' Creed

I believe in God, the Father almighty,
  creator of heaven and earth.

I believe in Jesus Christ, his only Son, our Lord,
  who was conceived by the Holy Spirit
  and born of the virgin Mary.
  He suffered under Pontius Pilate,
  was crucified, died, and was buried;
  he descended to hell.
  The third day he rose again from the dead.
  He ascended to heaven
  and is seated at the right hand of God the Father almighty.
  From there he will come to judge the living and the dead.

I believe in the Holy Spirit,
  the holy catholic church,
  the communion of saints,
  the forgiveness of sins,
  the resurrection of the body,
  and the life everlasting. Amen.

Irenaeus claimed that even in the midst of the variety of doctrines, the church, which was scattered across the world and worshiping in many languages, was unified in the faith. The Apostles' Creed provided apostolic continuity for a diverse church, consisting of different ethnic and linguistic groups yet holding to the shared faith.

Another creed accepted universally by Christians is the Nicene Creed. Established in 325 CE at the Council of Nicaea, the Nicene Creed defines what the church believes about the Triune God. The Roman emperor Constantine convened the meeting in Nicaea, addressing the bishops in Latin, with a Greek translation. Given that he spoke Latin, Constantine apparently had trouble following the theological debates in Greek. The impetus for the council was to address the theological debate, particularly in North Africa and the Eastern Mediterranean, over whether Jesus was equal to God or was first created by God. Arius (250–336 CE) emerged as the leader of the group that argued that Jesus was created (a doctrine known as Arianism), a position soundly defeated at Nicaea. The Nicene Creed, with additions by the Council of Constantinople (381 CE), corrected the heresies of Arianism about the incarnation.

### The Nicene Creed

We believe in one God,
  the Father almighty,
  maker of heaven and earth,
  of all things visible and invisible.

And in one Lord Jesus Christ,
  the only Son of God,
  begotten from the Father before all ages,
    God from God,
    Light from Light,
    true God from true God,
  begotten, not made;
  of the same essence as the Father.
  Through him all things were made.
  For us and for our salvation
    he came down from heaven;
    he became incarnate by the Holy Spirit and the Virgin
      Mary,
    and was made human.
    He was crucified for us under Pontius Pilate;
    he suffered and was buried.
    The third day he rose again, according to the
      Scriptures.
    He ascended to heaven
    and is seated at the right hand of the Father.
    He will come again with glory
    to judge the living and the dead.
    His kingdom will never end.

And we believe in the Holy Spirit,
  the Lord, the giver of life.
  He proceeds from the Father and the Son,
  and with the Father and the Son is worshiped and
    glorified.
  He spoke through the prophets.
  We believe in one holy catholic and apostolic church.

We affirm one baptism for the forgiveness of sins.
We look forward to the resurrection of the dead,
and to life in the world to come. Amen.

Even the vast majority of noncreedal churches—that is, those churches that do not recite a creed as a part of their weekly worship—endorse these confessions of faith. Therefore, the creeds proscribe beliefs and practices outside their scope. As Wilken notes, "Christian teaching does not lend itself to every possible opinion; it imposes limits that cannot be formulated in advance, but become evident over time. . . . Some differences could not be tolerated."[31] Christian teaching carried with it moral responsibilities that distinguished Christians from others. This teaching was aimed at effecting inner and outer transformation, the permanent hallmark of Christians in society ever since.

## Conclusion

To be a Christian does not require membership in a particular ethnic, racial, political, or economic grouping. Yet to be a Christian does mean a particular way of living, of following "the Way," Jesus Christ, and being regenerated by him. "Christian" is both a noun and an adjective. It is shortsighted to attach "Christian" to a thing, subject, or ideology as a sort of bounded unit that makes no room for ethnic and cultural diversity. Seeing "Christian" as both noun and adjective expresses the breadth of what it means to be Christian.

Of course, "Christian" refers to content, knowledge, and experience, since a Christian accepts certain beliefs and knowledge about God, the natural world, the state of humanity, and the self. In this sense, "Christian" is a noun that describes one whose identity is rooted in the Triune God and the work of Jesus Christ to provide new life. "Christian" also is a modifier, an adjective that denotes a change in direction that gives rise to that new life.

To some, "Christian" means sameness—for example, the same way of talking about God, the same style of clothing, worship, even

---

31. Wilken, *First Thousand Years*, 45–46.

architecture. The history of Christian missions demonstrates count-less occasions when recipients of the new faith followed the ways of the missionaries, appropriating mission culture rather than seeing Christianity through their own cultural lenses. One might defend the missionaries by arguing, "Didn't the apostle Paul write, 'In Christ Jesus I became your father through the gospel. Therefore I urge you to imitate me'?" (1 Cor. 4:16). Imitation has to be part of Christian formation, right? Yes and no. Yes, when it refers to following Jesus Christ; no, when it means making another's expression of Christianity the litmus test of genuine faith.

Christians lived in "the Way" of the Nazarene, Jesus.[32] They were followers of the Triune God attested to in the Bible, regenerated by God through the sacrifice of Jesus Christ, and filled with the Holy Spirit, who guided and comforted them. These peculiar people, called Christians, were not to be content with loving and serving one another. Their call and purpose were to spread the good news of salvation in Christ to every tribe and ethnic group worldwide. That mission is what we turn our attention to in the next chapter.

32. See, e.g., John 14:6; Acts 9:2; 19:9, 23; 24:22.

# 2

# Where Are Christians?

About 150 years ago, if you talked about Christianity, you would have been referring to a religious movement that was overwhelmingly European. Many countries were still in the throes of mostly European colonialism. Christianity was perceived as European. For many, to be European was to be Christian. European Christians discovered that the constellation of the "three Cs"— Christianity, commerce, and civilization—coalesced well to create a potent force that transformed societies, economies, and histories worldwide. European Christianity was part and parcel of the idea of "development," as Christian and non-Christian Europeans were occupying forces throughout much of Asia, Africa, Latin America, and Oceania.

Yet Christianity existed outside the Global North. Early Christians spread the gospel and lived in Africa and Asia. Christianity began in the Middle East. And in the first century Christianity had made many parts of Africa its home, with some of the greatest early theologians coming from that continent. Regardless of their early presence in Asia and Africa, the numbers of Christians in those regions were relatively small. Europe was the center of gravity of Christianity—its theological categories, financial resources, and cultural values being heavily European. The sheer force of European Christianity would alter the world.

This mattered immensely because European Christianity became the model of being Christian in much of the European-colonized world, from the Gikuyu of Kenya to the Quechua of Peru to the Batak of Indonesia. Along with the introduction of European Christianity came particular ways of expressing Christianity that were at times quite distinct from the local cultures of those receiving the faith. The history of encounter was uneven, with instances of acceptance and rejection of European forms. Massive negotiation between European Christianity and local Christianity created both commonalities and distinctions in the areas as diverse as theology and clothing.

European Christianity was the dominant form of the faith for many years. European Christians introduced many long-lasting influences on non-European peoples and cultures—for instance, European languages (e.g., English, French, Dutch) used to communicate the Christian faith; European theological interpretations of Christian categories of a vast array of concepts, such as "God," "sin," "forgiveness," and "grace"; European philosophical ways of thinking in the areas of epistemology, metaphysics, and ethics; and body regimes that encouraged European modes of hygiene, hairstyle, and household organization.

All this has changed. Over a period of a few decades, roughly between 1970 and 2020, the geographic distribution of Christianity changed dramatically. And with that change came increasingly different ways to interpret and express the faith. The change did not happen overnight, but it entailed a burgeoning of Christianity outside of the North Atlantic (i.e., North America and Western Europe), so much so that the numbers of Christians in the Global North were dwarfed by those in the Global South. This global shift was in part related to the growth of local Christian leadership during the period of decolonization and a dynamic process of partial decoupling of Christianity from direct colonial overlordship. During this period, Christianity was fraught with ambiguity as some Christians supported, while others resisted, colonial powers. It has been estimated that in 1970, about 41 percent of all Christians worldwide were from Africa, Asia, or Latin America. By 2020, this percentage is expected to approach 65.[1] Today, Christianity is the largest religion in the world. The religion is on every continent, and in nearly every nation. Today, if we think that Christianity is predominantly a "Western religion," our perceptions need to change. The fact is that although great influence remains in the West, numerically the faith is increasingly non-Western.

I will begin this chapter by tracing the early spread of Christianity, looking at the apostles, their mission, and postapostolic mission, and then providing snapshots of the current dispersal of Christianity around the globe. Following these historical reflections, I will discuss the relationship between population and influence and speak to the interconnected nature of Christianity.

The first usage of the term "Christian" was in the New Testament, and it meant "follower of Christ": "The disciples were called Christians first at Antioch" (Acts 11:26). The persecution of early Christians, beginning with the martyrdom of Stephen (Acts 7), led to their scattering throughout the Roman Empire and beyond. From the Roman Empire, Christianity spread to Europe and parts of Africa and later traveled on the ships of colonizers to territories in Africa, Asia, Latin America, and the Pacific. It has become the largest religion in the world today, with roughly 33 percent of the world's population identifying as Christian.

## The Apostolic Mission

Christianity began with a motley crew of disciples in the region of Palestine. From there it has become the tradition followed by roughly a third of the world's population. Along the way, Christianity transformed peoples, cultures, and economic and political systems with a sense of urgency from the start, fueled by the Spirit.[2] The message of

1. Gina A. Bellofatto and Todd M. Johnson, "Key Findings of Christianity in Its Global Context, 1970–2020," *International Bulletin of Missionary Research* 37, no. 3 (2013): 158.
2. It is worthwhile to note that prior to the emergence of Christianity, occurrences of the Greek terms *metanoeō* and *metanoia*, referring to a transformative change of heart, were rare. The terms appeared in the literature only 95 times from the eighth century BCE until the end of the first century BCE. In the first two hundred years

the breaking in of the gospel of Jesus Christ was geared toward every people group as its final destination. The Christian mission—the great sending of the church, the body of Christ as a sign and instrument of Christ on earth—started mostly in urban centers throughout the Roman Empire, such as Alexandria, Antioch, Ephesus, Sardis, Carthage, and Rome. The great missionary Paul started young churches, rather than "missions," to which he provided teaching and admonition through his presence and writings.[3] Far from being elitist, early Christians represented a wide variety of people, from fishermen to tax collectors, many of whom were of the common classes in the Roman Empire.

The disciples were referred to as "apostles," a Greek term that meant "one who is sent"; in the case of Christianity, an apostle is a messenger and ambassador who conveys the message of its sender, the Triune God, through God the Holy Spirit. Discipleship led to apostleship; following led to being sent. For these disciples, apostleship meant being witnesses, sealing their testimony through suffering. Each disciple suffered horribly for the sake of the kingdom of God.

The Gospel of Mark commences with Jesus's proclamation, "The time is fulfilled, and the kingdom of God is at hand; repent and believe in the gospel" (Mark 1:15 NASB [cf. Matt. 4:17]), affixing a missionary stamp on the very beginning of Christianity. This faith was not limited to a particular geography or ethnicity. The apostles, who received Jesus's teaching, were granted authority to cast out impure spirits, preach, and perform miracles (Mark 6:7, 30; Acts 2:43), as a testimony to the power of the resurrection of Jesus Christ (1 Cor. 15:7). The apostles provided leadership to the early churches. All, except for John, were brutally put to death.

The message that the apostles shared and for which they died was the proclamation of the kingdom of God, a message to turn from idols to worship the living God, and to trust and follow God through

---

of the Common Era, the terms occurred approximately twelve hundred times. See Guy D. Nave Jr., *The Role and Function of Repentance in Luke-Acts*, Academia Biblica 4 (Leiden: Brill, 2002), 39.

3. Roland Allen, *Missionary Methods: St. Paul's or Ours?* (Grand Rapids: Eerdmans, 1962).

Jesus Christ (Matt. 10:32). The scope of the call was universal, empowered by the Holy Spirit (Acts 1:8). By living by the Holy Spirit, Christians were filled with "love, joy, peace, forbearance, kindness, goodness, faithfulness, gentleness, self-control" (Gal. 5:22–23), virtues that shaped new communities worldwide.

### Who Were the Apostles?

Jesus started his mission with twelve disciples, along with several other men and women. After Jesus was betrayed by Judas Iscariot, Matthias was chosen as Judas's replacement. The reach of the disciples demonstrates that both Jewish and gentile communities were contacted. James, Peter, and John were apostles to the Jews (Gal. 2:9). Paul, a converted Jew who had led in the persecution of Christians until his dramatic encounter with the risen Christ (Acts 9:1–6), describes his own work as primarily among the gentiles, ministering in Jerusalem, Antioch, Cyprus, southern Asia Minor (Anatolia), Tarsus, Derbe, Lystra, Philippi, Corinth, Ephesus, Caesarea, Galatia, Macedonia, Tyre, and other locations.[4] Paul's three missionary journeys helped spread Christianity throughout much of the Roman Empire. Eventually, Paul was beheaded, having left an enduring legacy through his pastoral letters to the churches he established.

Peter, originally a fisherman, was called by Jesus and then sent from Jerusalem to Samaria and Antioch. Known as a passionate and outspoken disciple of Jesus, Peter was counted as the first bishop of Rome (i.e., pope), and the first patriarch of Antioch. He was crucified upside down at his request. Tradition says that Peter and Paul founded the church in Rome. They were both martyred in Rome around 66 CE, during the persecution of Christians under Emperor Nero.

Andrew, born in the village of Bethsaida on the Sea of Galilee and brother of Peter, was a fisherman by trade. Early church writers wrote that Andrew ministered in Asia Minor and preached along the Black Sea, ministering as far as Kiev, eventually becoming the patron saint of Ukraine, Russia, and Romania, among other locations. The

---

4. See, e.g., Rom. 1:5, 13–14; 11:13; 15:14–21; Gal. 2:1–10.

Romanian Orthodox Church claims that Andrew preached in the province of Dobruja, which he is said to have converted to Christianity. The 1320 Declaration of Arbroath, Scotland's Declaration of Independence, states that Andrew was instrumental in the conversion of Scotland to Christianity. Andrew's ministry later developed into the Patriarchate of Constantinople. Tradition says that Andrew traveled to Greece, where he was crucified.

Thomas, known as the doubter (see John 20:24–25), was most active in the area east of Syria. Tradition has him sailing to India, and eventually ministering in the present-day states of Tamil Nadu and Kerala, where he baptized many people and founded the Mar Thoma Nazranis Church. Thomas is revered as the patron saint of India. Tradition says that Thomas was martyred in 72 CE, being pierced through with spears by four soldiers at the location of today's St. Thomas Mount, outside of Chennai in southern India.

Philip, from the city of Bethsaida, preached in Asia Minor and Carthage in North Africa. Noncanonical books, such as the Acts of Philip, mention that Philip was sent with his sister, Marianne, and Bartholomew to preach in Greece, Syria, and Phrygia. This same source notes that while ministering in Asia Minor, where Philip converted the wife of a Roman proconsul, Philip was arrested and brutally put to death in retaliation, crucified upside down along with Bartholomew. Tradition holds that even from his cross Philip was preaching the gospel, and as a result, Bartholomew was released. Philip, too, could have been freed, but instead he insisted on dying on the cross. Some of these details, even the way in which Philip died, may be hagiographic.

Bartholomew, who is mentioned as one of the witnesses to Christ's ascension, traveled to India with Thomas, and to Armenia, Ethiopia, and Southern Arabia. Tradition says that Bartholomew was part of a group that convinced King Polymius, in the Roman province of Armenia, to embrace Christianity. It is believed that Bartholomew was flayed alive, thus he is often portrayed in statuary and art holding his own skin.

Thaddaeus, also known as Jude or Judas Thaddaeus (not to be confused with Judas Iscariot, the disciple who betrayed Jesus prior to his crucifixion), was killed by arrows in 65 CE in Beirut in the

Roman province of Syria. The Armenian Apostolic Church honors Thaddaeus and Bartholomew as its patron saints. Tradition holds that besides Armenia, Thaddaeus preached the gospel in Judea, Samaria, Syria, Idumea, Mesopotamia, and Libya.

James, a fisherman and older brother of John the apostle, ministered in Syria. A second James, the son of Alphaeus, was reported by the Jewish historian Josephus to have been stoned and then clubbed to death. Another tradition maintains that this James was crucified at Ostrakine in Lower Egypt.

Matthew, a tax collector, whose hometown was Capernaum, preached the gospel to the Jewish community before ministering in Persia and Ethiopia. Tradition says that Matthew was stabbed to death in Ethiopia.

Simon the Zealot, probably a Galilean, ministered in Persia, and possibly Armenia or Beirut, Lebanon, after ministering in Egypt. One tradition says that he was crucified in 61 CE in what is now Lincolnshire, England.

Tradition says that Matthias, who replaced Judas Iscariot, went to Syria with Andrew and was put to death by burning. While the Bible says little about Matthias, it notes that he was with Jesus from Jesus's baptism until his resurrection. Tradition says that Matthias died in 80 CE, having spread the gospel on the shores of the Caspian Sea and in Cappadocia.

John died a natural death from old age, after taking care of Mary, the mother of Jesus, and being exiled to the island of Patmos, where it is believed he wrote the book of Revelation.

Christianity started in a geographically widespread fashion throughout Asia Minor, South Asia, the Middle East, and Europe. By the time the apostles died, Christianity was clearly well on its way to becoming a global religion, and the seeds planted by the disciples and other Christians burgeoned into the largest religion in the world.

## What We Learn from the Postapostolic Mission

What enabled Christianity to spread so quickly throughout and beyond the Roman Empire? As we consider the broad themes below, keep in mind that what is happening on the ground is not a binary between centers and peripheries, between cosmopolitan centers and rural outliers. Instead, Christianity was more like a network, without a single command center, yet where particular regions exerted greater influence than others.

First, the *institutionalization and standardization* of Christianity enabled it to be transported across geographic, ethnic, and linguistic boundaries. Paul the apostle sent workers to minister to the younger churches he and others had started. As a result of this, "a network of Christians—linked together by correspondence and itinerant teachers like Paul—began emerging in the cities across the Roman empire."[5] Paul concentrated his work in certain strategic centers, mostly provincial capitals, the main centers for culture, commerce, and religion, with the expectation that from those metropolises the gospel would be communicated outward to surrounding towns.

Letters written in the second century by Ignatius, bishop of Antioch, a metropolis in ancient Syria, provide insight into early Christianity, showing that "the churches in Asia Minor were not isolated circles of believers existing independently of one another; they understood themselves to be a part of a larger body bound together in a mysterious spiritual unity."[6] Ignatius is credited with being the first one to use the term "catholic church" to refer to an organic fellowship, a single communion united to Christ.

Early Christian communities were directed both inward, toward their shared unity in Christ, and outward, toward the wider world, where they established new networks for fellowship and outreach. According to Wayne Meeks,

> The local groups of Christians not only enjoyed a high level of cohesion and group identity, they were also made aware that they belonged to a larger movement, 'with all who invoke the name of our Lord Jesus Christ in every place' (1 Cor. 1:2). In time they would invent a unique network of institutions to embody and protect this connection, and

5. Dana L. Robert, *Christian Mission: How Christianity Became a World Religion* (Oxford: Wiley-Blackwell, 2009), 13.

6. Robert Louis Wilken, *The First Thousand Years: A Global History of Christianity* (New Haven: Yale University Press, 2013), 29.

the resultant combination of intimate, disciplined local communities with a supralocal organization was a major factor in the social and political success of Christianity in the age of Constantine.[7]

The first Christian assemblies were limited in geographic scope in the Roman Empire, but they grew to become an institution called "church" (*ekklēsia*) that functioned as a fellowship for believers across ethnic and economic lines. By the fourth century, under Emperor Constantine, Christianity was legalized, allowing it to thrive in the Middle East, North Africa, and Asia. For the first few hundred years of Christianity, the spread of the religion relied on expanding urban networks and family connections.

Institutionalization entailed an increasingly centralized and hierarchical structure, where a bishop served as head in a particular city. New offices were developed—for instance, readers and acolytes (assistants) for Christian worship. Consensus at the meetings of bishops promoted the standardization of the faith, establishing the parameters of Christian orthodoxy. The role of bishops also contributed to the creation of creeds that helped to standardize the church's beliefs.

Second, Christianity spread through the *translation of the Bible* into indigenous languages. The common language of the Roman Empire was Koine (common) Greek, allowing early Christians to communicate the faith throughout the empire. The Septuagint, the Greek translation of the Hebrew Scriptures, was used extensively by Christians until about the fourth century. As Christianity expanded outside of the Roman Empire, Christians used local languages to convey the Christian story. Dana Robert writes, "The biculturality of the diaspora Jewish population, as exemplified by Paul himself— a Greek-speaking Jew—was essential for the expanded meaning of salvation that included both Jews and Gentiles."[8] We will revisit the significance of Bible translation in chapter 3.

Greek and Latin were the official languages of the Roman Empire. Greek had remained the language of many Christian communities, but some populations in the empire knew no Greek. Latin was the

---

7. Wayne A. Meeks, *The First Urban Christians: The Social World of the Apostle Paul* (New Haven: Yale University Press, 1983), 107.
8. Robert, *Christian Mission*, 13.

original language of the Romans. With the spread of Christianity throughout the Roman Empire, a Latin version of the Bible was needed in western regions of the empire so that Latin speakers could read and understand it. In 382, Pope Damasus commissioned the great biblical scholar Jerome to provide a translation of the Bible into everyday Latin. Jerome used the Septuagint Greek version of the Old Testament for his translation. Jerome's translation was called the Vulgate, the Bible used by the Western church until the Reformation in the sixteenth century. In the Middle Ages, though some discouraged the translation of the Old Testament, we see the emergence of portions of the Bible in Old English, High German, and Slavic languages, with the complete French Bible in the late thirteenth century. Martin Luther's Bible, in German, was published in 1521.

The Bible is the most translated book ever. Today, the entire Bible has been translated into 698 languages, the New Testament alone into more than 1,548 languages, resulting in 3,384 language groups having a portion of Scripture in their language.[9] In the following chapter I will discuss the importance of the Bible for Christians.

Third, Christianity expanded because it spoke of *a common history* for all peoples. In contrast to the view of history held by the other peoples of the ancient Near East, the Jews saw history as purposeful, culminating in a final judgment, rather than a repetitive cycle of birth and death. The fact that history's scope was universal, for all peoples and all times regardless of class, education, or culture, compelled people to join the new community. The Greeks and other Near Eastern civilizations thought that history followed a pattern of civilizational development, ascending and receding, in a never-ending cycle. The Hebrews, on the other hand, had a unique vision of history, recognizing that God's purpose and direction gave greater meaning to events and actions in the lives of communities. Christianity, an outgrowth of the Hebrew tradition, grafted cultures and histories onto the grand narrative of redemption. The challenge to Christian missionaries was to understand how particular histories were implanted onto the larger, universal trunk of redemption, a

9. "Scripture Access Statistics," Wycliffe Global Alliance, https://www.wycliffe .net/resources/scripture-access-statistics/.

story that began in Genesis with God's covenant with Abraham, childless at the time, yet through whom God promised to bless all peoples (Gen. 12:1–3; 17:9–14).

Fourth, Christianity advanced through the assertion of its *institutional power* and, at times, through a vision of human flourishing consisting of the three Cs: commerce, civilization, and Christianity. This was particularly the case during the period of European colonialism. At times, mission Christianity (the Christianity introduced by European missionaries) was implicated for having a view of the world based on a social evolutionary perspective, combined with the Enlightenment confidence that the West could help "less developed" nations. As European powers engaged in mercantile capitalism and then outright colonialism, mission Christianity, fueled by a desire and call to communicate the gospel "to the ends of the earth," frequently, but not always, coalesced with the power of European states to create global Christianity.

While mission Christianity bore a resemblance to other forms of colonial imposition, the history of encounter between mission Christianity and non-Western peoples was uneven; sometimes Christian missionaries displayed the ethnocentrism of their non-Christian compatriots, while at other times they were the only ones to defend the rights of indigenous populations. Consider Bartolomé de las Casas, a sixteenth-century Spanish colonizer who, upon seeing the treatment of Native Americans by Spanish colonists, became a Dominican friar and advocated before King Charles V, the Roman emperor, on behalf of the rights of the indigenous population.[10] Las Casas earned the reputation as the "Protector of the Indians," arguing forcefully for their dignity, and as a result was hated by Spaniards. While in Hispaniola in 1511, Las Casas recalled the words of his fellow Dominican António de Montesinos, as Montesinos's sermon, directed to the colonizers, shocked his listeners during his preaching on the Sunday before Christmas.

> "This voice," said he, "declares that you are in mortal sin, and live and die therein by reason of the cruelty and tyranny that you practice on these innocent people. Tell me, by what right or justice do you

10. See Gustavo Gutiérrez, *Las Casas: In Search of the Poor of Jesus Christ*, trans. Robert R. Barr (Maryknoll, NY: Orbis, 1993).

hold these Indians in such cruel and horrible slavery? By what right do you wage such detestable wars on these people who lived mildly and peacefully in their own lands, where you have consumed infinite numbers of them with unheard-of murders and desolations? Why do you so greatly oppress and fatigue them, not giving them enough to eat or caring for them when they fall ill from excessive labors, so that they die or rather are slain by you, so that you may extract and acquire gold every day? . . .

"Are they not men? Do they not have rational souls? Are you not bound to love them as you love yourselves?"[11]

Las Casas and Montesinos were not passive agents of the European colonial project. They contended against it in the face of the mistreatment of the indigenous people.

Another example of Christians who fought against social ills comes from those who opposed the African slave trade, such as William Wilberforce. Reflecting on the African continent, Andrew Walls notes, "The Evangelical-humanitarian confluence had provided the dynamism for William Wilberforce and his colleagues in their long battle for the abolition of the British slave trade, which they achieved in 1807."[12] As such, notes Walls, evangelicalism was "an implicit critique of contemporary British Christendom."[13]

Fifth, Christianity grew through the *activities of the Holy Spirit*, who was experienced through, for instance, dreams and visions, healings, and strength to endure suffering and persecution. Christians recognized that God worked through dreams, in the present as in the past, to communicate something about God and his purpose, and to establish the church.[14] Christians believe that God uses dreams and visions to communicate to Christians and non-Christians alike, often bringing those who do not know Christ into awareness of him

11. H. McKennie Goodpasture, ed., *Cross and Sword: An Eyewitness History of Christianity in Latin America* (Maryknoll, NY: Orbis, 1989), 12.

12. Andrew F. Walls, "An Anthropology of Hope: Africa, Slavery, and Civilization in Nineteenth-Century Mission Thinking," *International Bulletin of Missionary Research* 39, no. 4 (2015): 225.

13. Walls, "Anthropology of Hope," 226.

14. See, e.g., Gen. 15:1; 20:1–7; 28:10–17; 37:1–11; 40–41; Judg. 7:12–15; 1 Sam. 3; 1 Kings 3:5; Dan. 2; 4; Matt. 1:20; 2:13; 27:19; Luke 1:5–23; Acts 9:10; 10:1–6, 9–15; 11:1–6; 18:9–11.

as Lord and Savior. Jesus has appeared in the dreams of Muslims and Hindus, and many have followed him.[15] A corpus of literature testifies to the dynamic role of dreams and visions in the church around the world, particularly in Africa.[16]

Healing has been a major part of the proclamation of the gospel from the beginning of Christianity. Stories in the Bible tell of Jesus healing and instructing his disciples to do the same in order to manifest the kingdom of God (Matt. 10:8; Luke 9:2), demonstrating the power of God that breaks spiritual, emotional, and physical bondage. As both commoners and kings were healed, they were drawn to Jesus and the gospel he embodied. Indeed, Jesus's own popularity was based in large part on his ability to heal.[17]

Persecution and martyrdom have marked the history of Christianity since its inception, with the first believers enduring horrendous suffering for their faith. Christian martyrs are believers who have lost their lives prematurely, in situations of witness, as a result of human hostility. Demographers distinguish between "persecution," which entails some form of social or economic curtailment, and "martyrdom," which means being killed because of one's Christian faith or witness. The spread of Christianity is closely connected to Christian persecution and martyrdom. For example, in the first century, Stephen's martyrdom led to the scattering of Christians, where they

15. See, e.g., P. Y. Luke and John B. Carman, *Village Christians and Hindu Culture: A Study of a Rural Church in Andhra Pradesh, South India* (London: Lutterworth, 1968), 181; Nabeel Qureshi, *Seeking Allah, Finding Jesus: A Devout Muslim Encounters Christianity* (Grand Rapids: Zondervan, 2014), 18, 296, 332; Bilquis Sheikh, *I Dared to Call Him Father: The Miraculous Story of a Muslim Woman's Encounter with God* (Grand Rapids: Chosen, 1978), 28–33. Lausanne World Pulse Archives notes the well-documented phenomenon of people coming to Christ from a Muslim background because of dreams and visions of Christ: "More Than Dreams: Muslims Coming to Christ through Dreams and Visions," https://www.lausanne worldpulse.com/perspectives-php/595/01-2007. See also the video stories of five Muslims who had dreams or visions of Christ: *More Than Dreams*, http://morethan dreams.org/.

16. See, e.g., Nelson Osamu Hayashida, *Dreams in the African Church: The Significance of Dreams and Visions Among Zambian Baptists*, Currents of Encounter 13 (Amsterdam: Rodopi, 1999); Adrian Hastings, *The Church in Africa, 1450–1950* (New York: Oxford University Press, 1994), 510.

17. See, e.g., Matt. 8:16; 12:15; 14:14, 36; Mark 3:10; 6:56; Luke 4:40; 9:11; John 5:11; 6:2.

spread the word of Jesus to their fellow Jews in places such as Phoenicia and Cyprus and especially the great metropolis of Antioch on the Orontes (Acts 11:19).[18]

Persecution continues to be a part of Christianity to this day.[19] In fact, in November of 2017, German chancellor Angela Merkel acknowledged that Christianity is the most persecuted religion in the world. And she was correct. According to a recent publication by Rupert Shortt, religion editor of *The Times Literary Supplement*, over the course of the last millennium the problem of Christian persecution has worsened: "200 million Christians (10 percent of the global total) are socially disadvantaged, harassed or actively oppressed for their beliefs."[20] Regarding martyrdom, for the ten-year period from 2000 to 2010, it has been estimated that one million Christians were martyred, an average of 100,000 annually.[21]

## Clippings from around the World

What happened to Christianity in the postapostolic period, after the death of the disciples?[22] Christianity was caught in a flurry of ma-

18. Wayne A. Meeks, *The Moral World of the First Christians* (Philadelphia: Westminster, 1986), 109.

19. See, e.g., Paul Hattaway, *China's Christian Martyrs* (Oxford: Monarch, 2007).

20. Rupert Shortt, *Christianophobia*, http://www.civitas.org.uk/pdf/Shortt_Christianophobia.pdf, viii. These figures are based on reports from the Pew Forum and the Evangelical World Alliance. See also Rupert Shortt, *Christianophobia: A Faith under Attack* (Grand Rapids: Eerdmans, 2013). The *Catholic Herald* also notes, "Christians today face worse persecution than at any time in history" ("Christians Facing Worst Persecution in History, Report Says," *Catholic Herald*, October 12, 2017, http://catholicherald.co.uk/news/2017/10/12/christians-facing-worst-persecution-in-history-report-says/). See also Thomas Schirrmacher, *The Persecution of Christians Concerns Us All*, 3rd ed., WEA Global Issues 5 (Bonn: Verlag für Kultur und Wissenschaft, 2018), https://www.iirf.eu/site/assets/files/91406/wea-gis_05_thschirrmacher-persecution_of_christians_3rd_ed.pdf.

21. Todd M. Johnson and Gina A. Zurlo, "Christian Martyrdom as a Pervasive Phenomenon," *Society* 51, no. 6 (2014): 680.

22. For an overview of the early Christian history that focuses on locations and cultural contexts of Christian expansion, see William Tabbernee, ed., *Early Christianity in Contexts: An Exploration across Cultures and Continents* (Grand Rapids: Baker Academic, 2014).

neuverings for control and influence of mostly European state power over non-Western lands and peoples. The role of Christianity in this mix was complicated, sometimes benefiting from state power and other times opposing it. Below, in the brief retelling of the expansion of Christianity, you will see that "Christianity is not only the largest religion in the world; it also is the least regionalized. . . . There is no region without significant numbers of Christians."[23]

As we survey Christianity around the globe, keep in mind that these snapshots are concise and do not account for the breadth and scope of Christianity in each region. They merely provide glimpses of massive and complicated interactions between cultures, societies, religions, histories, and political systems. What is important to recognize in these short overviews is that Christianity engages all aspects of culture and society in unpredictable ways, at times aligning itself with the power of government and military and other times becoming a persecuted minority religion. The changes brought by the faith throughout its history led to transformations of cultures and societies. What mediated those transformations ranged from colonial ships to literacy, yet what was common throughout its history was that disparate peoples, histories, and cultures were grafted onto the history of redemption portrayed in the story of Christianity. The Bible as the Word of God and the message of Jesus as Savior of the world were common themes that would unify Christians worldwide.

### Africa

African Christianity began in Egypt in the middle of the first century, when the apostle Mark became the first bishop of the Orthodox Church of Alexandria in about 43 CE. Several important Africans were early church leaders who shaped Christianity. For example, Origen, Athanasius, and Cyril of Alexandria, Tertullian and Cyprian of Carthage, and Augustine of Hippo were massive figures in the early church, contending against threats to Christianity presented by a variety of heretical groups. People spend their entire lives studying

---

23. Rodney Stark, *The Triumph of Faith: Why the World Is More Religious than Ever* (Wilmington, DE: ISI Books, 2015), 16.

these monumental figures and the enduring legacy they have left to Christianity.

As Islam, which emerged in the Arabian Peninsula in the early seventh century, advanced through North Africa, Catholic and Coptic Christianity were nearly decimated. Yet the Coptic form of Christianity survived. Islam overtook Christian communities beginning in 711 from Morocco to the India-Pakistan border, but Christianity remained robust in the Ethiopian Empire and persisted in pockets throughout North Africa. Heather Sharkey notes that by the time Islam entered North Africa and the Middle East, Christians in the region "were already evincing the doctrinal and communal pluralism, or sectarianism, that became one of world Christianity's defining features."[24]

In the fifteenth century, Christianity arrived in sub-Saharan Africa with the arrival of the Portuguese. At that time, Portuguese seafarers also traveled around to West Africa, introducing Christianity to the region in part through Portuguese commercial voyages, where Roman Catholic priests accompanied the expeditions.

In the eighteenth century, the Moravian Church of Denmark and the Society for the Propagation of the Gospel attempted to spread Christianity, but with little success.

Under the influence of the Protestant Great Awakening in Britain, the nineteenth-century missionary activities of the Wesleyan Methodist Society, the Basel Mission, and the Bremen Mission successfully established Christianity in Africa. Likewise, in the nineteenth century, when France colonized Algeria and Tunis, Catholicism was reignited mostly because of French colonizers. The interior of the continent had less contact with mission Christianity until the nineteenth century, when missionaries, in part motivated by an antislavery crusade, ministered alongside their fellow European colonists.

Christianity penetrated East Africa in the mid-nineteenth century, with missionaries requiring a total break with indigenous traditions. New forms of clothing and architecture, as well as education and healthcare, were introduced as part and parcel of Christianity.

24. Heather J. Sharkey, "Middle Eastern and North African Christianity: Persisting in the Lands of Islam," in *Introducing World Christianity*, ed. Charles E. Farhadian (Malden, MA: Wiley-Blackwell, 2012), 9.

The African continent has experienced explosive growth of Christianity in the twentieth and twenty-first centuries, due mostly to the proliferation of African Initiated Churches (AICs), which often opposed the European dominance of Christianity on the continent. From the 1930s, the East African Revival birthed numerous Christian movements that focused on spirituality, renewed faith, and political engagement.[25] With the entrance of mission Christianity on the continent came literacy, education, healthcare, and commerce. Yet, despite this growth, the forces of globalization coming from the West pressed in on daily life. "In the burgeoning urban cities and townships, ethnic diversity, frail and fragile family structures, and the absence of processes of initiation militated against effective cross-generational cultural transmission. . . . But this was a world whose primary cultural references were Western. Hollywood films, for example, provided models for modes of dress and sources of names, and those that were not submerged in the world of gangs were increasingly drawn into Western forms of education and culture."[26] The emergence of classical Pentecostal churches in the twentieth century fueled further growth and expanded Christianity's transnational connections, creating a network of Christianity worldwide. Mainline Protestant churches experienced renewal as "they offered a theological response that corresponded to the religious and spiritual needs of Africans.[27]

The African continent has seen tremendous growth of Christianity, particularly compared to that of Islam. According to Lamin Sanneh, "Muslims in 1900 outnumbered Christians by a ratio of nearly 4:1, with some 34.5 million, or 32 percent of the population. In 1962, when Africa had slipped out of colonial control, there were about 60 million Christians, with Muslims at about 145 million. Of the Christians, 23 million were Protestants and 27 million were

25. See, e.g., Kevin Ward and Emma Wild-Wood, eds., *The East African Revival: History and Legacies* (Burlington, VT: Ashgate, 2012).

26. Ann Bernstein, "Globalization, Culture, and Development: Can Africa Be More Than an Offshoot of the West?," in *Many Globalizations: Cultural Diversity in the Contemporary World*, ed. Peter L. Berger and Samuel P. Huntington (New York: Oxford University Press, 2002), 195.

27. Opoku Onyinah, "African Christianity in the Twenty-First Century," *World & World* 27, no. 3 (2007): 309.

Catholics. The remaining 10 million were Coptic and Ethiopian Orthodox."[28]

By the beginning of the twenty-first century, the number of Christians had increased sixfold to over 380 million, more than the Muslim population (in 1900, there had been only 9 million Christians). The median age of Christians in sub-Saharan Africa is 19 years old, while in North Africa and the Middle East it is 39. According to a 2015 report, over 2 million Muslims have become Christians on the continent.[29] Today, the majority of sub-Saharan Africans are Christian.

### Asia

Since Christianity has its roots in Palestine, the earliest form of Christianity is Asian. Paul and the apostles introduced Christianity throughout the Levant—that is, the Eastern Mediterranean—establishing the faith in major urban centers, such as Jerusalem and Antioch. The apostles communicated Christianity far outside of the Roman Empire—for instance, Thomas traveled to India and Andrew to Russia. In South Asia, Christianity was connected to the church in Syria and Persia, its worship influenced by Syrian liturgy. Armenia (301) and Georgia (327) were the first nations in the world to declare themselves Christian.

Nestorian Christianity, considered heretical because of Nestorius's view of Christ, was introduced into China as early as 635. When Catholic missionaries appeared in China in the sixteenth century, they were surprised to discover remnants of Nestorian Christianity, such as a Nestorian stone erected in 781 that documented 150 years of Christianity in China prior to the arrival of the Jesuits. The Franciscan John of Montecorvino arrived in Beijing in 1294, introducing Catholicism to China. Yet the permanent Catholic presence began with the efforts of Matteo Ricci, an Italian Jesuit, in 1601.

28. Lamin Sanneh, *Whose Religion Is Christianity? The Gospel beyond the West* (Grand Rapids: Eerdmans, 2003), 15.

29. Duane Alexander Miller and Patrick Johnstone, "Believers in Christ from a Muslim Background: A Global Census," *Interdisciplinary Journal of Research on Religion* 11, no. 10 (2015): 17.

The state of Kerala, in southern India, boasts of being the first Roman Catholic diocese in Asia (1329), while European Franciscans, Dominicans, and Jesuits began ministering in the Philippines beginning in the sixteenth century.

When in 1549 the Jesuit Francis Xavier entered Japan, at the request of the converted samurai Anjirō, whom he met in India, Xavier established Catholic communities there, working through the local feudal lords (*daimyō*). Under the Tokogawa Shogunate (1600–1868), when Japan was unified, Christianity was banned and heavily persecuted due to Japanese suspicion that Portugal had planned to colonize Japan by using Christian missionaries. Hidden Christians (*Kakure Kirishitan*) kept the faith alive, even if underground.

Protestant mission efforts began in the early eighteenth century when German Lutherans Bartholomäus Ziegenbalg and Heinrich Plütschau introduced Protestantism to the eastern coast of South India, in the Danish colonial territory of Tranquebar, becoming the first Protestant missionaries in the history of the church.

Korea's history with Christianity is unique, claiming to have been self-evangelized by Koreans who traveled to China to learn Christianity from the Chinese writings of Matteo Ricci, who, in the sixteenth century, had translated Western works into Chinese and Confucian classics into Latin. Ricci and fellow Jesuits encouraged the Chinese to retain their customs, such as their ancestral rites of veneration.

Several literati (intellectuals) became Christians. The "rites controversy," a debate about the practice of ancestral rites, pitted the Vatican against the Chinese imperial court and Korean authorities. The Vatican condemned ancestral rites since they believed such practices to be the worship of ancestors, while Chinese and Korean authorities embraced the rites as simply an act of veneration. This conflict led to the cessation of Jesuit work in China in 1724 when the Chinese emperor outlawed Christianity, giving rise to a period of Christian persecution. In 1784, Korean Yi Sŭnghun was baptized in Beijing and then returned to Korea to baptize others.

Protestantism grew vigorously in Korea beginning in the late nineteenth century, under the influence of missionaries John Ross, Horace N. Allen, Horace G. Underwood, and Henry G. Appenzeller, each representing his own sending denomination.

In 1899, the Russian Orthodox Church arrived in the Korean Peninsula, ministering to both Russian expatriates and Koreans. Korean Christians actively promoted the 1915 March First Independence Movement, a series of protests resisting Japanese rule over Korea. After the Korean War, Protestants and Catholics fled to South Korea. In the second half of the twentieth century, Korean Protestantism grew rapidly, in part because of the role played by Christian Koreans in political independence. In South Korea, evangelical Protestants have predominated in numbers and political, cultural, and religious influence.

The Protestant movement in China began with the arrival of Robert Morrison to Guangzhou (1807). After the two Opium Wars (1839–42 and 1856–60), Christianity continued to exist in China but was hindered because it was associated with Western nations that had contended against China. Under Chinese communism (1949) and the Cultural Revolution (1966–76), Christianity waned and church properties were seized by the state. But the Three-Self Patriotic Movement, a government-controlled Protestant denomination, allowed for Chinese Christianity to grow, even though many Protestants and Catholics continued to practice their faith in unregistered house churches. The Chinese Catholic Patriotic Association (CCPA) has oversight over China's Catholics, with bishops not recognized by the Vatican.

After 220 years of Japanese isolation from the West and gunboat diplomacy of the United States, Japan (in 1854) received merchants and missionaries, both Catholic and Protestant, eventually becoming more tolerant of the Christian faith. During World War II, Protestant missionaries were sent back to the United States, and Christianity declined significantly. Today, Christians make up less than 1 percent of the Japanese population.

Christianity is the majority religion in Russia, Cyprus, Philippines, East Timor, Armenia, and Georgia, with large minority populations in South Korea, China, India, Vietnam, Indonesia, Singapore, Hong Kong, Malaysia, Lebanon, and Syria. Since 2010, Christianity is the fastest growing religion in Asia, with an average rate of growth of 2.1 percent annually.[30] In 1970, there were 95 million Christians (4.5

---

30. Todd M. Johnson and Gina A. Bellofatto, "Key Findings of Christianity in Its Global Context, 1970–2020," *International Bulletin of Missionary Research* 37, no. 3 (2013): 159.

percent), with growth to 450 million (9.2 percent) forecast by 2020.[31] Rodney Stark noted a significant decline in "irreligion" in China since 2001, with 93 percent of Chinese giving their religion as "none" in 2001 and 77 percent responding the same in 2007.[32]

Each of these regions in Asia offers a fascinating look into the nature of Christianity vis-à-vis culture, society, and history. I could only offer a quick look here, with the hope that this will whet your appetite for further reading.

### Latin America

Latin American Christianity traces back to the coming of Christopher Columbus, who famously arrived in Santo Domingo in 1492 with Spanish seamen who were Christian. On a second journey, in 1493, an ecclesiastical delegation joined the expedition with the aim of ministering to locals in the New World. The ensuing years witnessed the arrival of small groups of Catholic orders: Franciscans, Dominicans, Jesuits, and Augustinians. Thirty-five years after their initial arrival, there were eight hundred Catholic missionaries in Mexico alone. These early missionaries carried with them building equipment, books, and small objects from Europe to trade with Native Americans. Itinerant priests went from village to village, baptizing, teaching, and often defending the Native Americans against abuse at the hands of European colonists. Spaniards were culpable for cruelty against Native Americans, and large sections of the Native American population were obliterated through violence or disease. Catholic missionaries established "reductions" (*reducciones*), city-states or settlements where Native Americans were assigned to live and labor together, sometimes forced to do so. The Catholic encounter in South America was portrayed in Roland Joffé's film *The Mission*, which depicted the violent conflict between Spanish and Portuguese government power against that of the Catholic priests.

In the mid-sixteenth century, Protestants settled in northern Venezuela, and a French colony was established in Brazil, where they introduced

---

31. Johnson and Bellofatto, "Key Findings," 159.
32. Stark, *Triumph of Faith*, 147.

pastors from Geneva. In the early seventeenth century, Dutch colonists started plantations in northeastern Brazil, establishing mission posts and translating the Bible. In the early nineteenth century, the first Protestant missionary arrived in Spanish America, James Thomson of the British and Foreign Bible Society. Thomson established a system of education and distributed thousands of Bibles in Spanish.

According to 2010 figures from the Pew Research Center, there are 531 million Christians in Latin America and the Caribbean, which is 90 percent of the overall population. Brazil alone has 173 million Christians. Latin America is overwhelmingly Catholic, but the numbers of Catholics have declined substantially to 69 percent in 2014, with a concurrent rise in the numbers of *Evangélicos*, a trend similar among Latin Americans in the United States.

### North America

Christianity was introduced to North America by European colonizers beginning in the sixteenth and seventeenth centuries, with the Spanish, French, and British launching Roman Catholicism while Northern Europeans launched Protestantism. The earliest forms of Protestantism were Anglican, Baptist, Congregationalist, Presbyterian, Lutheran, Quaker, Mennonite, and Moravian. In 1565, Roman Catholic Spanish colonizers were the first Europeans to arrive in what would later be known as North America. By 1776, due to Protestant settlers fleeing the Church of England, Protestant denominations emerged in the form of Puritanism, and by the time of the American Revolution (1765–83), the English colonies were almost entirely Protestant. Various European peoples controlled territories that would later become the United States, with the Spanish establishing colonies in Florida (1513) and the southwest region of America (mostly Roman Catholic) and the French in Detroit, St. Louis, Mobile, Biloxi, Baton Rouge, and New Orleans, with a strong presence along the Mississippi River. The British entered New England, establishing the Massachusetts Bay Colony (1629) as a place for Puritan Protestants, and Virginia (1619), where the Church of England was introduced. Roger Williams, a strong advocate of the separation of church and state, founded the Colony of Rhode Island as a refuge from the Puritans.

Jesuit settlers introduced Catholicism to the Province of Maryland (1634). The Russian Orthodox Church, mostly through Russian traders, was established in Alaska in the eighteenth century. The first American movement to abolish African slavery in the colonies came in 1688 when Dutch and German Quakers in Pennsylvania wrote and circulated a two-page letter condemning slavery.

In the early eighteenth century, the massive revival movement known as the Great Awakening occurred, beginning in the northeastern part of the territories. Led by Jonathan Edwards and George Whitefield, this Protestant revival (re)introduced an evangelical sensibility to Christian faith, with preaching that aimed at personal conversion through intense personal experience with God rather than through what some perceived as cold and rigid ritual or ceremony. There were many lasting results of the Great Awakening, but two were particularly salient: (1) it revived Protestantism's emphasis on personal conversion and ongoing life with God, and (2) it gave rise to some of the greatest educational institutions in the United States, which were started as missionary training schools (e.g., Harvard, Yale, Brown, William and Mary, Princeton).

The Second Great Awakening, beginning in 1790, was more consciously outward looking in terms of extending invitations and preaching messages geared toward people outside the church. Many who became Christian during the Second Great Awakening ardently opposed slavery, such as Benjamin Titus Roberts, whose opposition to slavery contributed to his founding of the Free Methodist Church in 1860.

By the mid-nineteenth century, the Roman Catholic Church became the country's largest denomination, mostly through immigration from Ireland, Germany, Italy, and Poland. Catholic numbers increased in the twentieth century through immigration from Philippines and Latin America. In the early twentieth century, American Pentecostalism arose out of the pietism and holiness movements beginning with the Azusa Street Revival (1906) in Los Angeles, California. American Pentecostalism gave rise to several new global-reaching churches, such as the Assemblies of God.

Eastern Orthodoxy, historically consisting of ethnic groupings (e.g., Armenian, Greek, Assyrian), also grew in the United States in the past hundred years as Orthodox immigrants arrived in the United States. For example, Greek, Armenian, Russian, and Serbian Orthodox churches began with the arrival of diasporic communities.

The religious history of North America has had at least one striking feature: "a tendency, proceeding over several centuries, to greater and greater levels of freedom in matters of conscience. The logical consequence of this freedom has been the creation, through both choice and happenstance, of a religious environment that, with time, has grown ever more *diverse* and *pluralistic*."[33]

Christianity has declined in the United States in recent years, dropping from 78.4 percent in 2007 to 70.6 percent in 2014. As with the other regional glimpses of Christianity, these events are only a small piece of a wider and deeper story of Christianity.

### Europe

Europe and Asia share a regional boundary, with overlapping regions in Asia Minor—for instance, with present-day Armenia and Turkey. In the 50s and 60s CE, the apostle Paul wrote letters to followers of Jesus Christ, the Way, in Galatia, Macedonia, Greece, and Rome. The Edict of Milan (313 CE) guaranteed freedom of religion throughout the Roman Empire. By 380 CE, Christianity was legalized, and by the late tenth century, most of Europe had become Christian. As the Roman Empire collapsed in the late fifth century, Christian missionaries took their faith outside the empire into the northern regions. In the seventh century, Islamic caliphates conquered much of the eastern part of the Roman Empire, with a dramatic decrease of the numbers of Christians in the Byzantine Empire.

In 1054, the Great Schism, when Western (Catholic) and Eastern (Orthodox) churches split, shattered the communion between Roman Catholicism and Eastern Orthodoxy for hundreds of years, until the last two popes, Pope Benedict XVI (2005–13) and Pope Francis (2013–present), were more forthright about possibilities of Christian unity across ecclesial lines. By the end of the eleventh century,

---

33. Kevin J. Christiano, "Christianity in North America: Changes and Challenges in a Land of Promise," in Farhadian, *Introducing World Christianity*, 139.

over half of the ancient Christian world was conquered by Muslims. The Crusades (mostly the eleventh through thirteenth centuries), a response to Muslim expansion in the Holy Land and eastern Mediterranean, were blessed by the popes and were presented by the church as a means of redemption and expiation for sins. From the fifteenth to the eighteenth century, Christianity expanded throughout the world during European colonialism. With the emergence of the Protestant movement in the sixteenth century, European mission Christianity consisted of Roman Catholic, Eastern Orthodox, and Protestant forms. Roman Catholic mission societies in Europe, such as the Jesuits, Augustinians, Dominicans, and Franciscans, started missions to communicate Christianity to indigenous populations.

In the Middle Ages, as Roman education declined, bishops utilized their cathedrals to provide an educated clergy, establishing schools in Canterbury (596), Rochester (604), and York (627). Beginning in the eleventh century, cathedral schools established their own institutions, such as the University of Paris (ca. 1150), University of Bologna (1088), and University of Oxford (1096). Christianity significantly impacted education, medicine, and science since the church provided the basis for modern Western education and scientific investigation. Jesuits actively led the effort to develop modern science. Catholics and Protestants spearheaded the establishment of hospitals and social welfare organizations as well as influencing economics, politics, literature, arts, and marriage and family. Currently, immigration is drastically altering the religious landscape of Europe, where Christianity grew between 1970 and 2010 but now is in decline.[34]

### Oceania

Christianity in Oceania, the Pacific island region comprising Melanesia, Micronesia, Polynesia, Australia, and New Zealand, began under the influence of Spanish and Portuguese expeditions seeking raw materials and markets during the Industrial Revolution in Europe in the eighteenth century. This coincided with the burgeoning trade with China beginning in the late eighteenth century, when Europeans

34. Johnson and Bellofatto, "Key Findings," 160.

combed the Pacific looking for goods and trading glass beads, whisky, and muskets for sandalwood, sea cucumbers, pearls, and turtle shell, which they in turn sold to the Chinese for tea, silk, and porcelain. European missionaries accompanied these trade expeditions, ministering to Pacific Islanders and teaching them about the Triune God, Christian family life, and new body regimes, encouraging them to dispense with their local practices of cannibalism, war, drinking kava, and chewing betel nut.

The expansion of Christianity moved from Polynesia, to Micronesia, and finally to Melanesia. In 1770, the British explorer Captain James Cook first observed indigenous Australians, sparking European interest in the region. In 1797, members of the London Missionary Society arrived in Tahiti. The missionary Rev. John Williams introduced Protestantism to the Cook Islands (1823) and Samoa (1830). Methodists arrived in Tonga (1822) and Fiji (1835). French Catholic missionaries arrived in Polynesia in 1834, where they competed with Protestants for influence over the Pacific Islanders, with backing from the French protectorate, which allowed Catholicism to flourish there.

Christianity is the predominant religion in Oceania. With 92.1 percent Christian in Melanesia, 93.1 percent in Micronesia, and 96.1 percent in Polynesia, the Pacific has one of the highest percentages of Christians in the world. Australia and New Zealand have lower percentages of Christians, with 47.5 percent of New Zealanders and 52.1 percent of Australians declaring some form of Christianity. Secularization and immigration have impacted the growth of Christianity in Oceania since 1970. High rates of Chinese and Indian immigration are changing Oceania's religious landscape; Buddhists in Oceania grew at 4.35 percent per year between 1900 and 2000 (from 0.1 percent to 1.5 percent of the population), with a growth rate between 2000 and 2020 of 4.04 percent (up to 2.4 percent of the population in 2020).[35]

Immigration, secularization, and the growth of non-Christian religions have both dramatically challenged the church as well as

---

35. Todd M. Johnson and Gina A. Zurlo, *World Christian Encyclopedia*, 3rd ed. (Edinburgh: Edinburgh University Press, 2020), 18.

provided opportunities to engage in Christian witness. The history of Christianity illustrates that theology emerges from a context of mission as Christians encounter others unfamiliar with Christian faith. Some Christians find that the stories of that encounter make up the most inspiring and heartening moments in Christianity, as well as being the springboard for innovative thinking in theology and the arts.

Historians and anthropologists have built their entire careers by studying the growth of Christianity in just one of these areas. Laying out the history of the expansion of Christianity is a massive task, too immense for our purposes here. It is impossible to capture the entire history of Christianity worldwide in a few pages, but these brief overviews give us a sense of the global expansion of Christianity and hint at its complicated relationship with various features of culture, society, religion, commerce, the arts, and politics.

## The Numbers

Statistically, Christianity is no longer a "Western religion" since the majority of Christians now live in the Global South. But in terms of influence, the Global North still has massive impact worldwide. When we try to understand the presence of Christianity in various regions of the world, it is tempting to rely too heavily on numbers and demographic changes in our interpretation. Numbers are helpful, but alone they can mask deeper realities. In the last few decades, most books and articles that discuss Christianity have focused on demographic shifts in the numbers of Christians and their distribution worldwide, noting the swing in the center of gravity of Christian growth from the Global North to the Global South. We ought to resist basing our understanding of Christianity worldwide solely on numerical shifts, since numbers alone can be misleading when disconnected from events on the ground. Certain centers of Christianity have more influence than others. With this in mind, let us start with the demographics and then pull back the curtain and see what we can learn.

Demographers of religions tell us that as of 2010 there were approximately 2.2 billion Christians around the world, making it the largest religion in the world.[36] Although Christianity extends throughout the world, its history and presence vary immensely, in large part because of forces (e.g., spiritual, economic, political, religious) that impede or accelerate its growth and impact. Christian witness is empowered by the Holy Spirit, and thus it has grown even when Christians were excluded from society, employment, or family, or when they lost everything, even their lives.[37]

Let us consider the numbers. According to the *World Christian Encyclopedia,* in 2020 Christianity consisted of Roman Catholics (1.24 billion), Protestants (585 million), Orthodox (292 million), and independents (391 million). Charismatics/pentecostals (644 million) and evangelicals (387 million) are movements within the four major traditions of Christianity: for example, a Christian can be a Catholic charismatic or an independent evangelical charismatic.[38] Christians in 2020 consisted of approximately 667 million people in Africa, 383 million in Asia, 565 million in Europe, 612 million in Latin America, 268 million in North America, and 27 million in Oceania.[39] In 2020, the countries with the most Catholics were Brazil (150 million) and Mexico (116 million), with Africa experiencing the greatest Catholic growth during the twentieth century (4.32%).[40] Independents, those Christians who do not self-identify with the other major traditions (Orthodox, Protestant, or Catholic), occur in huge numbers in the Global South (314 million), consisting for instance of "house church movements in China (55 million), Kimbanguists in the Democratic Republic of Congo (12 million) and the Universal Church of the Kingdom of God in Brazil (7.5

36. "Christian Population by Country," Pewforum.org, http://www.globalrelig iousfutures.org/religions/christians. See also Stark, *Triumph of Faith,* 15; Todd M. Johnson and Kenneth R. Ross, eds., *Atlas of Global Christianity: 1910–2010* (Edinburgh: Edinburgh University Press, 2009), 7.

37. The history of Christian growth is replete with stories of suffering and persecution for those who become Christians, reminding us that Christian conversion was not always for material or political gain. See, e.g., Miles J. Stanford, *Fox's Book of Martyrs: A History of the Lives, Sufferings, and Deaths of the Early Christians and Protestant Martyrs,* ed. William Byron Forbush (1926; repr., Grand Rapids: Zondervan, 1967).

38. Johnson and Zurlo, *World Christian Encyclopedia,* 8–18.

39. Johnson and Zurlo, *World Christian Encyclopedia,* 6.

40. Johnson and Zurlo, *World Christian Encyclopedia,* 21.

million).[41] Orthodox Christian traditions, which usually have close connection between church and ethnicity, have decreased, dropping from 7.2 percent of the global population in 1900 to 3.7 percent in 2020, partly due to the Armenian Genocide and twentieth-century Communism.[42] In 2020, Protestants, who consist of such families of churches as Lutheran, Reformed, Baptist, Methodist, Brethren, Salvationist, and Friends, stood at 23.2 percent of Christianity, with expected massive growth in Africa where they were only 1.6 percent of all Christians in 1900 and are projected to reach 55 percent by 2050.[43] Also in 2020, the Global South was home to 86 percent of all charismatics/pentecostals in the world.[44] You might be surprised to learn that "the largest Charismatic movement today is the Catholic Charismatic renewal, found in significant numbers mainly across Latin America."[45] In terms of gender, world Christianity has been described as a "woman's movement"; it is estimated that women make up more than two-thirds of Christian missionaries.[46]

Among the regions with the lowest percentages of Christians in the world is the Middle East, the birthplace of Christianity, where the number of Christians continues to decline as a result of their terrible persecution and oppression at the hands of Islamist groups (e.g., Al-Qaeda, ISIS, ISIL). Christians were 13 percent of the Middle East population in 1900, but in 2020 that number declined to 4 percent.[47]

Andrew Walls makes a good point when he argues that Christianity is unique vis-à-vis geography because Christianity is less territorial than other religions; Christianity relativizes geography rather than absolutizing it, sanctifying all geography as equally important. Christianity has become a more geographically diverse religion over the past one hundred years, becoming less concentrated in Europe and more distributed throughout the Americas, Asia-Pacific, and sub-Saharan Africa.[48]

41. Johnson and Zurlo, *World Christian Encyclopedia*, 22.
42. Johnson and Zurlo, *World Christian Encyclopedia*, 23.
43. Johnson and Zurlo, *World Christian Encyclopedia*, 24.
44. Johnson and Zurlo, *World Christian Encyclopedia*, 26.
45. Johnson and Zurlo, *World Christian Encyclopedia*, 26.
46. Johnson and Zurlo, *World Christian Encyclopedia*, 26.
47. Johnson and Zurlo, *World Christian Encyclopedia*, 5.
48. Johnson and Zurlo, *World Christian Encyclopedia*, 5.

Although it is important to understand the figures and demographic changes, we ought to avoid being overly distracted by the role of geography in Christianity, since the great center of Christianity is the person and mission of Jesus Christ, not geography. Because of Jesus Christ, geography itself is transcended. In Richard Bauckham's words, "It is the particular human person Jesus, crucified and exalted, who draws all people and to whom all people are drawn. . . . Jesus, the Messiah for all people, the Saviour for all people, has all the temporal and geographical particularity of a genuinely human person."[49] Bauckham notes that the Gospel of John shows that Jesus draws people to himself in a centripetal image that combines with the centrifugal image of the disciples being sent out by Jesus to continue his mission (John 20:21). Let us keep in mind that Jesus, not geography, is the center of Christian faith and movement.

## A Networked Faith

Although Christianity ebbs and flows around the world, certain geographic centers have disproportionate influence over the rest. The mistake, when looking just at the demographic shifts, is to put statistics before the empirical reality—in other words, to put the statistical cart before the empirical horse. Instead of prioritizing statistics in our interpretation of Christianity, it is crucial to see the relationship among Christian communities around the world, their connectivity across time and space.

In concert with the academic approach to studying Christianity, which often overlooks nonempirical, spiritual forces, we need to remember that Christians credit the Spirit of God for animating the movement of Christianity. Thus, the utterly unique nature of Christianity as a movement of the Spirit of God needs to be figured as part of the reason for Christianity's expansion, for "the wind blows wherever it pleases" (John 3:8).

49. Richard Bauckham, *Bible and Mission: Christian Witness in a Postmodern World* (Grand Rapids: Baker Academic, 2003), 79.

Rather than possessing a common geographic center, the movement of Christianity was tied fundamentally to a community that, in the words of Richard Bauckham, "manifest[ed] God's presence in its midst by its life together and its relationship to others."[50]

This networked movement began with the apostles at the very start of the faith. The Gospel of Matthew contains the story of Jesus sending out his disciples. They were to travel light: take no silver, gold, or copper, no bag for the journey or extra shirt or sandals or staff (Matt. 10:9–10). We can imagine this disparate crew walking down dusty roads, sailing over rough waters, sleeping in small houses in villages far from their homes, having faith that a worthy person would take them in. To communicate the gospel they employed the same techniques as their contemporaries, such as letter writing and rhetorical strategies. Likewise, subsequent to the work of these early apostles, missionaries employed nearly every conceivable means to communicate the gospel.

Yet the rise of global connectivity introduced a new dynamism that transformed the world, and Christianity as well. In our contemporary world, missionaries no longer travel light as they did when Jesus sent out his disciples (Matt. 10:1–11). They carry cell phones and the latest Apple and PC products to enhance communication with mission centers and families back home. Bible translation software quickens the process of learning and translating the Bible into indigenous languages.

Global connectivity has profoundly transformed Christianity and its relationship to locations worldwide since the modern period.[51] Today's world is interconnected in unparalleled ways through circulatory paths resulting from globalization that creates networks worldwide—for instance, in the areas of finance, culture, entertainment, and religion.[52] Yet the world, though interconnected, is linked

50. Bauckham, *Bible and Mission*, 77.

51. I use the terms "modernity" and "globalization" to refer to broad social, political, economic, and religious movements beginning with European colonization, development of capitalism, bureaucracy, and technology, and their attending institutions. Globalization involves, at least, the extension of these forces and institutions across national boundaries with a scope and speed hitherto unknown.

52. See, e.g., Kerry Ward, *Networks of Empire: Forced Migration in the Dutch East India Company* (Cambridge: Cambridge University Press, 2009), 41.

in uneven ways. What travels on those circulatory paths and the directions from which they travel reveals that the flow of ideas, objects, and preferences is not even across the world. Christianity too has circulated via the paths laid down by the forces of globalization, networks of organizations and institutions providing conduits for its passage.[53] Some observe that Christianity itself was a major instigator of globalization since its reach was universal.

Thus liturgies, creeds, denominational pronouncements, polity decisions, theological affirmations, ecumenical confessions, architectural styles, musical instrumentation and melodies are ideas that are flowing globally from one Christian community to others. One can just as easily find music by Chris Tomlin, Matt Redman, and Third Day and books by T. D. Jakes, Joni Eareckson Tada, Anne Graham Lotz, Joel Osteen, and Pope Francis in Indonesia, Singapore, or Johannesburg, as in London, Los Angeles, or Toronto.

The exercise of the Roman Catholic Church's magisterium, the church's teaching authority, influences well over a billion people stretching over all seven continents. American Catholic bishop Robert Barron, auxiliary bishop of the archdiocese of Los Angeles and known for his Word on Fire ministry, is one of the world's most popular Catholics on social media, with over 1.5 million followers on Facebook. Opus Dei, the most influential organization of the Roman Catholic Church today, began in Spain in 1928 and now has members in more than ninety countries.

The Alpha Course, an evangelistic course originating from Holy Trinity Brompton, a Church of England parish in London, is offered in 169 countries and 112 languages, with over twenty-seven million people having taken the course.[54] Rick Warren's book *The Purpose Driven Life* has sold over thirty-four million copies and is one of the best-selling nonfiction books in history, after the Bible.[55] Tim LaHaye's Left Behind series, with over sixty-five million sold in over twelve language translations, grew into a massive industry of apocalyptic

53. Many argue that Christianity always gives rise to particular economic (e.g., capitalism) and political (e.g., democracy) systems.

54. "About Alpha," Alpha International, https://www.alpha.org/about/.

55. See Zondervan's website for the book: https://www.zondervan.com/978031 0329060/the-purpose-driven-life/.

movies, video games, albums, and graphic novels. Church pronouncements, translated Bibles, books, and polity transform people's attitudes toward one another, the nation, God, sexual behavior, work,
child rearing, and economics. They also introduce new preferences
for individual modern identities.

Conceptualizing Christianity as a totality of networks with some
regions exerting more influence than others within the massive grid
allows us to recognize shifting patterns of "connection, dissolution,
and reconnection."[56] While Christianity in the Global South is having
some influence on the North, Christianity in the North has inordi-
nate influence on that in the South. More work needs to be done to
understand these "geographies of connection" that not only provide
connection worldwide but today also enable the transportation of
Christianity as embodied witness.[57]

56. Here I borrow the helpful language of Ward, *Networks of Empire*, 10.
57. See Alan Lester, *Imperial Networks: Creating Identities in Nineteenth-Century South Africa and Britain* (New York: Routledge, 2001), 5.

# 3

# Why Is the Bible So Important to Christians?

The film *Black Robe* portrays the seventeenth-century ministry of a young French Jesuit priest, Laforgue, as he seeks to convert the Algonquin people of Quebec, Canada, in the dead of winter. In the midst of his spiritual journey, Father Laforgue has a fascinating encounter with two Algonquin leaders, one of whom is called Chomina. The Algonquin call Father Laforgue "Black Robe" because of his clothing, a black habit. A scene opens with Father Laforgue scribbling notes in his notebook. Chomina and a fellow Algonquin approach Laforgue as the priest writes with a quill pen.

Looking intrigued, Chomina inquires of Laforgue, "Black Robe, what you do?" Laforgue, looking up, responds, "Making words," returning his eyes to the page on which he is inscribing notes.

Responding inquisitively, Chomina ponders, "You not speak."

Black Robe knows that the Indian does not understand what is happening, so Black Robe says, "I will show you. Tell me something. Something I do not know."

With an expression of bewilderment, Chomina states matter-of-factly, "My woman's mother die in snow last winter."

Father Laforgue records the words in his notebook, the two Algonquin careening in to view what must appear as a strange event since they had never seen writing. After writing the phrase, the priest stands up and walks, with Indians following, to a fellow Frenchman, Daniel, living among the Algonquin.

The priest hands Daniel the notebook. Daniel takes up the book and reads out loud, "Last winter, Chomina's wife's mother died in the snow."

Immediately, Chomina grabs the book, absolutely bewildered, and exclaims, "What tells you?" shocked about the possibility of communicating with just scribbles on paper.

The priest responds, "I have still greater things I can teach you."[1]

Can you imagine recognizing for the first time the incredible power of conveying a thought and knowing that those ideas and sentiments were portable across distances? What would that do to your understanding of space and time, since your stories could travel without your permission, be misunderstood, or be cherished? Father Laforgue was correct: because of the power of the written word, he had still greater things to teach.

The written word transports readers differently than the spoken word. For literate societies, writing is part of the taken-for-granted world, part of the rhetorical environment that surrounds us. Walk down any street and try to count the number of words that bombard you. Add to that the number of words in your private, public, and virtual life, seeking to convince, encourage, disrupt. Where do these words take us?

John Milton wrote, "Books are not absolutely dead things."[2] The Bible is a book of words, yet unlike any other book. The Bible is the most popular book in the world and the most translated book ever. Written over a period of 1,500 years and by numerous authors, it communicates its message through poetry, history, and theology, all geared toward conveying the story of God's creative action and relationship with human beings. Its writing was inspired by the Holy

---

1. *Black Robe*, directed by Bruce Beresford (1991; Beverly Hills, CA: MGM, 2001), DVD.

2. From John Milton's speech "Areopagitica," in *Complete Poems and Major Prose* (1957; repr., Indianapolis: Hackett, 2003), 720.

Spirit, rather than being merely a compilation of the thoughts of human authors. Many mistakenly think of the Bible as *the* answer book, thumbing through it like an instruction manual for life. While there might be some benefit to this arbitrary approach to find encouragement or challenge, the Bible is more than just a book of answers. Trevor Hudson reminds us that the Bible is a book in which God invites us to listen to questions that God has *for us*, so that each of us can enter into a deep conversational relationship with God and know God more intimately.[3] "Where are you?" "What are you doing here?" "Do you understand what I have done for you?" The Bible does provide answers to our most enduring questions, but through it God also asks us questions directly.

Today's Christians confront three metanarratives: the Enlightenment, Marxism, and postmodernity—the "universal cultures"—which seek to strip the Bible of its authority and insert themselves as ultimate framing devices for understanding the world. Biblical authority, however, does not wane in the face of philosophical trends. Historian Jaroslav Pelikan concludes that biblical authority, rather, functions in the interaction of the community of faith and the Holy Spirit: "In Christianity the authority of a Bible . . . has constantly been in the process of being normatively interpreted and then reinterpreted, ever since its various component parts, as the community of faith affirms, were first written down by the writers and prophets under the inspiration of the Spirit of God."[4]

In Miroslav Volf's view of Scripture, "True, fresh water can come from other sources too—reason, tradition, and experience, to name the three most frequently visited wells. Yet everything in theology that is specifically Christian finally derives from and is, in one way or another, measured by the content of the Scriptures, above all the Scriptures' witness to Jesus Christ."[5]

In order to answer the question that this chapter asks—Why is the Bible so important to Christians?—I will first discuss the nature

---

3. Trevor Hudson, *Questions God Asks Us* (Nashville: Upper Room, 2008), 12.

4. Jaroslav Pelikan, *Whose Bible Is It? A History of the Scriptures through the Ages* (New York: Viking, 2005), 79.

5. Miroslav Volf, *Captive to the Word of God: Engaging the Scriptures for Contemporary Theological Reflection* (Grand Rapids: Eerdmans, 2010), 11.

of the Bible. What is the Bible? Christians affirm that the Bible is the Word of God, revealed to its authors through God the Holy Spirit. The Bible, then, is unlike any other book. Second, we will consider how the Bible was put together in a process called canonization. You might be surprised to learn that the Bible was assembled in part as a measure of protection against various heresies (i.e., false teachings). Third, what does the Bible say? Perhaps this is the most significant question as we learn about the importance of the Bible. What is the content of the Bible? What is its message, and why is it so appealing to some and, perhaps, repulsive to others?

Fourth, we will look at the Bible as a translated text; the Bible is available in more languages than any other book. What are the implications of the Word of God entering cultures with a new message that might at once judge and celebrate elements of that culture and our lives? Finally, since we cannot separate the Bible from culture, we take a look at the Bible in various cultural contexts. It is not surprising that different cultural contexts will emphasize different aspects of the biblical message, yet all Christians affirm the Bible as revealed by the Triune God.

## What Is the Bible?

For the first one hundred years of the church's existence, Christians read almost exclusively from the Old Testament as their sacred Scripture. The books that would later become the New Testament existed, with most having been written before the end of the first century, but had not yet been elevated to the status of Scripture. Even early church leaders of the patristic period, such as Barnabas, Justin, and Clement of Rome, when referring to Scripture, were referring to the Hebrew Scriptures (i.e., Old Testament) rather than the corpus of material that would become the New Testament.

The word "Bible" is derived from the Greek term *biblia* ("books"). In early Christianity, "Bible" was used to designate the entire sacred collection of books we know today. Therefore, the Bible is a collection of books. The words of the Bible are inspired by God (2 Tim. 3:16) through the Holy Spirit (2 Pet. 1:20–21). Those words are Spirit-breathed yet mediated by human authors whose person-alities and different perspectives are evident throughout each book. Christians affirm that the Bible is "special revelation," since it com-municates information about God, human beings, and our world that cannot be deduced from our observations in our daily lives.

The content of this special revelation includes the identity of God as consisting of a triune nature (three persons of Father, Son, and Holy Spirit sharing one essence); Jesus Christ having suffered for our sins, died on the cross, and risen again to conquer death to make a way for us to be healed from sin and have a relationship with God; Christ returning in the future in power and glory to judge all nations; God being holy and yet loving us so much that he would send Jesus Christ, God's self-disclosure, to die for our sins. The Bible speaks about love and invites us to love rightly. As such, the Bible conveys the grand narrative about God, creation, human life, rebellion, inner and outer states of our humanity, and the environment.

The Bible consists of sixty-six books written over a period of 1,500 years by dozens of authors from different geographic locations, cultures, and educational backgrounds. The Bible was penned on the continents of Asia, Africa, and Europe and in three languages (Hebrew, Aramaic, and Greek). The Old Testament was originally written in Hebrew and Aramaic and the New Testament in Koine Greek, the vernacular languages of much of the ancient Near Eastern world. At least six different literary genres appear in the Bible: law, historical narrative, poetry, wisdom, apocalyptic, and epistles (i.e., letters). The Bible is divided into Old and New Testaments, the Old Testament written prior to the birth of Jesus Christ, the New Testa-ment after his death and resurrection.

The Old Testament, a collection of Jewish writings, consists of thirty-nine books. The New Testament consists of twenty-seven books containing the events in the life, ministry, death, and resur-rection of Jesus Christ, the beginning of the Christian church, and the letters to the churches founded by the apostles.

The New Testament describes a "new covenant" between God and human beings whereby people can be saved from sin through the death and resurrection of Jesus Christ (Luke 22:20; 2 Cor. 3:6; Heb. 9:15). A covenant is a legal contract, in this case between God and human beings. The Bible has been handed down through the generations of Christians and continues to have the function of teaching, admonishing, and encouraging believers in all cultures throughout time.

Regardless of the various debates about the unity and diversity of the Bible itself, the single scarlet thread of redemption woven through the entire Bible is the history of God's action to save people from the power of sin and the curse of the law (Gal. 3:13) through Jesus Christ (Rom. 3:24; Col. 1:14). This story of redemption encompasses all particular histories (e.g., economic, social) and is not, therefore, a separate story apart from other histories but is the largest frame within which to see all stories.

The Bible is more than just a metanarrative—an overarching interpretation of the world's events—for it does more than tickle our imagination or cognitive framing of the world. It does not simply convey a story that encompasses all other stories, even though the Bible does give meaning to those stories. The Bible is truth, but even then it does more than convey truth as an abstract idea, for it tells of the possibility for us to be healed of our broken relationship with God and one another. This is how the Bible refers to itself: "For the word of God is alive and active. Sharper than any double-edged sword, it penetrates even to dividing soul and spirit, joints and marrow; it judges the thoughts and attitudes of the heart" (Heb. 4:12). The Bible is timeless and powerful, since it exposes human sin, disordered loves and ambitions, and is a life-giving Word that communicates about God and God's love for us. Yet there are limits. Christians are not to worship the Bible; that would be bibliolatry. As the Protestant Reformers put it, the words of the Bible reveal the Word, Jesus Christ.

## How Was the Bible Put Together?

Emerging from a Jewish and Greco-Roman environment, Christianity struggled against the destructive heresies launched by Gnosticism, Marcionism, and Montanism. Gnosticism mixed ideas from docetism, a dualistic perspective that split the world of spirit from that of matter, an idea that deeply challenged the early church from the church's inception. The word "gnostic" comes from the Greek word "to know." Gnostics claimed that they possessed higher, esoteric knowledge (*gnōsis*) of God based on mystical insight rather than the Bible, and they believed that Christ was a spirit, not human. Bodies were considered evil, and spiritual realities were good. The Gnostic Gospels, for instance, presented Jesus as a luminous presence, revealed through secret knowledge.

A second threat to early Christianity came from the Marcionites. Based on the teachings of Marcion of Sinope, the Marcionites argued for the existence of two Gods, a wrathful God of the Old Testament, called the Demiurge, who created the world, and a loving, merciful God of the New Testament, revealed in Jesus Christ. Thus, Marcion argued that the Old Testament was not authoritative for a Christian. Similar to the Gnostics, Marcion held a docetic view of Jesus that Jesus was not truly a human but only appeared to be human.

A third major heretical threat to early Christianity came from Montanus, a Christian convert who declared himself not only possessed by the Holy Spirit, which in itself may not sound unusual for a Christian, but also to have received special and final revelations—for instance, about a rigid code of ethics and belief in the imminent return of Jesus Christ. Montanus's heretical and ecstatic prophecies included the view that Christ was going to return soon to establish the new Jerusalem in the vicinity of the town of Pepuza in Phrygia, Asia Minor.

Can you imagine if a new pastor preached that Jesus was only a luminary light rather than having a real body, that there were two Gods, that the pastor held final authority in all matters of the church, or that the pastor's insight surpassed the authority of the Bible, even the words of Jesus? The presence of these heresies created crises among Christians, forcing churches to create antiheretical instruments that could protect Christianity from the influence of these new movements.

None of these diffusely organized groups were ever embraced by a majority of Christians in the first two centuries of Christianity. However, the popularity of Gnosticism and the teachings of Marcion and Montanus forced Christians to clarify and formulate their beliefs. In the first fifty years of Christianity, all that was required for admission to Christian fellowship was repentance, affirmation that Jesus was Lord, baptism, and reception of the Holy Spirit. Within the onslaught of early heresies, however, there emerged a call for greater definition of what would guide Christian thinking and living. The church at large responded to the heresies in a surprisingly uniform way.

Toward the end of the second century, the larger Christian community moved toward a fixed and more uniform organization, calling itself the "catholic" (i.e., universal) church.[6] During this time, the church developed antiheretical instruments that served as mechanisms to confront unorthodox groups. The most important of these instruments were the development of the canon and creeds; the emphasis on apostolic succession, which affirmed the uninterrupted transmission of spiritual authority from the apostles to bishops and other church leaders; and the rise of apologists, who defended Christianity from heresy.

Christians use the term "canon" (*kanōn*), meaning "rule" or "measuring stick," to affirm the texts that were revealed and inspired by God and serve as authoritative for all people. "Canon" refers to books that contain the rules and norms of Christian faith. For others, the Bible might be seen as a book of moral teachings (e.g., Jeffersonian Bible), a set of myths, or merely writings of human origin.

What, then, is Christian Scripture? Scripture is writing, which seems obvious. One has to be literate to read it. Scripture is especially sacred since it points to ultimate reality. Scripture is also authoritative; it is the most authoritative and final court of appeal in religious, social, and cultural matters. As such, Scripture regulates personal and public life. Finally, Scripture is by nature both heterogeneous, since it contains books written by numerous authors, and unified.

Those who reject the sacred nature of Scripture might even have a high view of the Bible—that is, "it is moral teaching, nevertheless"— but do not necessarily believe it to be authoritative in their lives or their communities. In 1979, the Yale Old Testament scholar Brevard

---

6. "Catholic" was first used by Ignatius of Antioch (second century) to describe the church, in the Platonic sense of "universal" rather than particular. Gradually, the term "catholic" was used to describe "orthodox"; thus, in large part, the beginning of the Roman Catholic Church coincides with the appearance of these various methods to confront heresy.

Childs published an Old Testament overview, *Introduction to the Old Testament as Scripture*, whose title ("Scripture") was scandalous, particularly during the height of the biblical-criticism movement, in which many scholars deconstructed the text of the Bible without seeking to convey its integrity as a set of documents inspired by God.

Furthermore, the Bible is a "closed canon" because orthodox Christians (e.g., Roman Catholic, Eastern Orthodox, Protestant) believe that public revelation of God is complete and that no other text can have the same authority as the Bible. This view contrasts with an "open canon" perspective, which believes that new revelations can occur and, therefore, the canon can be enlarged with the inclusion of these new revelations.[7]

Although the Bible is a closed canon, each of the major branches of Christianity emphasizes different passages according to its theological traditions. Generally, Eastern Orthodox Christians have a special connection to John's Gospel and Letters; Roman Catholics have an affinity for the Gospel of Matthew and later New Testament Letters, and Protestants have historically fastened onto Paul's Letters. In addition, there are some differences in the lists of books that have been included in the Bible, according to the various churches.

Catholic, Eastern Orthodox, and Protestant Christians recognize the following books of the Old Testament: Genesis, Exodus, Leviticus, Numbers, Deuteronomy, Joshua, Judges, Ruth, 1–2 Samuel, 1–2 Kings, 1–2 Chronicles, Ezra, Nehemiah, Esther, Job, Psalms, Proverbs, Ecclesiastes, Song of Songs, Isaiah, Jeremiah, Lamentations. Catholics and Eastern Orthodox Christians include the books of Tobit, Judith, 1 Maccabees, 2 Maccabees, Wisdom (of Solomon), Sirach, Baruch, Additions to Daniel, and Additions to Esther. Eastern Orthodox Christians include 1 Esdras, 3 Maccabees, 4 Maccabees, Prayer of Manasseh, and Psalm 151. Russian and Ethiopian Orthodox Christians include 2 Esdras. Ethiopian Orthodox Christians include Jubilees, Énoch, and 1–3 Meqabyan.

---

7. For example, the Church of Jesus Christ of Latter-day Saints believes in an open canon. As new revelations are received by the president of the Latter-day Saints (Mormons), who is also referred to as the Seer and Prophet, those revelations will be published in their sacred text, *Doctrine and Covenants*, believed to have canonical authority.

Why was the canon of Scripture so important? The New Testament canon was a crucial instrument that the church used in its struggle against heresy. During the first centuries of its existence, the Christian community found it necessary to make a distinction between the various documents, some heretical, used in individual Christian communities. By doing so, the church would be in a better position vis-à-vis the rest of the world and heretical movements, being unified on the foundation of its authority.

From their beginning, Christians understood the Old Testament as Scripture, revealed by God. Following the death and resurrection of Jesus Christ, however, Jesus's disciples, Paul, and other early Christians also wrote letters addressing Christian communities throughout the Roman Empire, teaching and admonishing them. These letters, called "epistles," were read in Christian gatherings, along with passages from the Old Testament. The Gospels and Paul's Epistles were highly valued, but they did not, at first, have scriptural authority. By the middle of the second century, the Gospels were read in the services in Rome, together with the Old Testament prophets.

Yet there were many letters and other writings read by Christian communities throughout the Roman world. These were not written by the disciples, though some had the name of a disciple of Jesus as author. All had additional, and sometimes unorthodox, information about Jesus, his life, and the early Christian community. These Apocryphal Gospels were among the writings that failed to make it into the New Testament.[8]

The process of canonization that gave rise to the final form of the Bible consisted of several criteria. The first criterion for deciphering which texts were canonical was apostolic authority. Canonical writing had to have been written by an apostle or church authority (e.g., Paul), affirming the authorship as coming from a direct follower of Jesus Christ who was "sent forth" with the gospel (e.g., Matthew,

8. There are over forty Apocryphal Gospels, including the Gospel of Thomas, the Gospel of Peter, the Gospel of Nicodemus, the Gospel of Bartholomew, the Gospel of Judas, the Gospel of Mary, and the Gospel of Philip. In the Apocryphal Gospels, we learn, for instance, that Pontius Pilate converts to Christianity, that Jesus departs the tomb supported by two massive angels, that Jesus had sex with Mary Magdalene, and that young Jesus gave life to clay pigeons and made them fly away.

John, Paul, Peter) or by someone under apostolic authority (e.g., Mark, Luke).

A second criterion for canonization was theological consistency. Given the theological conflicts that emerged in the second century, doctrinal content had to be weighed against the apostolic writings. This process was not without debate, since there were many books that claimed to have been written by an apostle. The only way to determine their authenticity was to compare the content of their teaching to books already held to be genuinely apostolic in theological content. For instance, the Gospel of Peter and the Gospel of Thomas were not permitted in the final canon, despite having the names "Peter" and "Thomas" attached to them, due to theological inconsistency with recognized apostolic documents.

The third main criterion in the process of canonization was scriptural usage by prominent Christian churches throughout the Roman Empire. In terms of the Gospels, Antioch promoted the Gospel of Matthew, the province of Asia Minor (i.e., western Turkey) used the Gospel of John and the Gospel of Luke, and Rome used the Gospel of Mark. Only gradually was universal assent given to the twenty-seven books that now comprise the New Testament.

## What Does the Bible Say?

The centerpiece of the Bible is the gospel, which in Lesslie Newbigin's view is distinguished from Christianity. The gospel is the enactment of the facts of what God has done, whereas Christianity is "what we have made of those facts."[9] That is, expressions of Christianity change, but the gospel remains the same. It is gospel that sets Christianity apart from any other religion. All world religions have sacred texts, sacred places, sacred objects, and models of pristine purity. Yet there is no message in any other religious tradition that is like the gospel.

9. Lesslie Newbigin, "Pastoral Ministry in a Pluralist Society," in *Witnessing Church: Essays in Honour of the Rt. Rev. Masilamani Azariah, Bishop of Madras*, ed. Chris V. Theodore (Madras: Christian Literature Society of India, 1994), 149.

The Bible says that God created the world and loves human beings. The self is not king. Nor is any political or economic system. Nor is any particular culture or ethnicity. Furthermore, idols have no power (Isa. 44:6–20; 45:1–21). In the Bible, God says, "I am the LORD, and there is no other; apart from me there is no God" (Isa. 45:5).

"Gospel" means "good news" and refers to a good announcement. Although the term "gospel" was used prior to the rise of Christianity, the biblical writers used the term to refer to the "good news of salvation" that through the life, death, and resurrection of Jesus Christ, human beings can be reconciled to God their Creator and have peace with God and assurance of salvation—this is the message of Christianity. The gospel, then, is foremost about Jesus: "Now, brothers and sisters, I want to remind you of the gospel I preached to you, which you received and on which you have taken your stand. By this gospel you are saved, if you hold firmly to the word I preached to you. Otherwise, you have believed in vain. For what I received I passed on to you as of first importance: that Christ died for our sins according to the Scriptures, that he was buried, that he was raised on the third day according to the Scriptures" (1 Cor. 15:1–4).

The noun *euangelion* ("gospel") appears over seventy times in the Greek New Testament and is thus a major theme, for the gospel both announces and brings salvation (Rom. 1:16; Eph. 1:13) and gives believers hope (Col. 1:23). "Gospel" also refers to the entire teaching and work of Jesus Christ: "The beginning of the gospel of Jesus Christ, the Son of God" (Mark 1:1 NASB). The book of Romans makes clear that the gospel is "the power of God that brings salvation to everyone who believes" (Rom. 1:16). As such, the gospel is of divine origin, and its scope is universal, intended to be communicated to everyone.

The gospel is about God, who loves and saves. Tim Keller says, "The gospel is not moral conformity, which is religion, nor is it self-discovery, which is secularism. The gospel is something else altogether—a grid through which we see the world. There are three results of the gospel: the restructuring of our hearts, the removal of our sin, and the reversal of our values."[10] Paul insisted that there is

10. Tim Keller, "The Gospel," September 25, 2005, https://www.youtube.com /channel/UCQmUmqrMGfnesNpdL7T282Q.

but one true gospel (Gal. 1:8), but he communicated that gospel in a variety of ways. To the Greeks, who were steeped in philosophy, Paul spoke about the "foolishness" of the cross, and he juxtaposed that to the wisdom of Christ's salvation; to the Jews, Paul underscored the "weakness" of the cross, and then he shared the gospel as true power (1 Cor. 1:22–25).[11] The gospel is the climax of the biblical metanarrative, the story of redemption that runs through the entire Bible. That grand narrative of redemption can be summarized in a variety of ways, but perhaps the most popular is through the four acts of creation, fall, redemption, and restoration.

*Act 1: God creates.* In the first few chapters of the Bible we learn that God created everything—and there was peace, *shalom* (Gen. 1). The world was created and populated with human beings to have a relationship with God, enjoy God's creation, worship God, and flourish. This garden of Eden was a paradise where all of humanity's needs were met.

*Act 2: Human beings fall.* The tragedy was that God created a paradise full of natural beauty, a place where human beings would be at peace, and yet human beings were dissatisfied. The Bible says, "And the LORD God commanded the man, 'You are free to eat from any tree in the garden; but you must not eat from the tree of knowledge of good and evil, for when you eat from it you will certainly die'" (Gen. 2:16–17).

Adam and Eve were tempted by the crafty serpent, who appears and speaks to Eve: "'"Did God really say, "You must not eat from any tree in the garden"?' . . . 'You will not certainly die,' the serpent said to the woman. 'For God knows that when you eat from it your eyes will be opened, and you will be like God, knowing good and evil'" (Gen. 3:1, 4–5). Adam and Eve ate the forbidden fruit, yet God still loved them, which is illustrated by the fact that God looks for them in the garden after their disobedience: "But the LORD God called to the man, 'Where are you?'" (Gen. 3:9). Their rebellion resulted in physical and spiritual death. All forms of life were cursed, fallen from their originally intended goodness (Gen. 3:14–19).

11. Tim Keller, "The Gospel in All Its Forms," Acts29.com, December 12, 2008, http://www.acts29.com/tim-keller-explains-the-gospel/.

This is when sin entered creation, and the time when human beings were indelibly marked by sin in all subsequent generations. Because of God's holiness, human beings were separated from God. In the Greek New Testament, "sin" means "to miss the mark." It is a failure, an error, an offense. The term was originally used in archery to describe when someone shooting an arrow missed the mark of the target. Furthermore, sin is ubiquitous, "For all have sinned and fall short of the glory of God" (Rom. 3:23). As a human race, we naturally miss the mark; we have fallen from what is good and life-giving. We have been infected by sin, falling short of our original purpose. In biblical terminology, sin refers to godlessness, injustice, wickedness, oppression, unjust deeds, unrighteousness, and a breach of a relationship.

There are two aspects of sin: subjective and objective. The subjective side of sin reflects our actions and intentions. When we do the right thing, we avoid sin. When we are kind, generous, and humble, we are avoiding the opposites, the sins of envy, greed, and pride, as though what we do and the state of our intentions can increase or decrease the sin in our life. The objective side of sin, however, goes much deeper because this aspect of sin is fundamentally a part of our human condition. There is nothing on a subjective level that we can do to eradicate it, since sin's objective nature is indelibly marked onto our DNA. All the Bible studies, prayers, and other "good works" cannot eliminate the objective nature of sin. We need an "efficacious grace" that is sufficient to deal with our objective sin, rather than just its subjective aspect.

Augustine (354–430 CE), a famous Roman African theologian whose insights shaped much Roman Catholic and Protestant theology, argued that the fall entailed the fall of the human volition—that is, the will to choose God. Thus, we as a human race were left deformed, unable to reconcile with God again, and our hearts were turned away from God. Augustine was careful to mention that in the post-Eden world, we still had the ability to choose, for instance, what we wear and where we travel. Yet our ability to choose God and to live harmoniously with God was irrevocably damaged. It is helpful to point out that just like creation, which entailed all things, the fall too was all-encompassing. Everything fell: our ambitions, desire, bodies, minds, emotions, cultures, and philosophies. We cannot save ourselves from our condition since sin enslaves (John 8:34). The Bible teaches us that we need a savior who can set us free. Otherwise, we will never have peace.

*Act 3: Christ redeems.* In the Bible we learn that Jesus Christ is the promised Messiah and Son of God, the self-disclosure of God who came to earth in human form (Rom. 1:3–4). The good news of the gospel is that Jesus Christ, the Messiah and Son of God, paid the price for our sin. He promises to set us free from the bondage of sin: "Jesus said, 'If you hold to my teaching, you are really my disciples. Then you will know the truth, and the truth will set you free. . . . Very truly I tell you, everyone who sins is a slave to sin. Now a slave has no permanent place in the family, but a son belongs to it forever. So if the Son sets you free, you will be free indeed'" (John 8:31–32, 34–36).

Why would God not leave us on our own, without any help? "God demonstrates his own love for us in this: While we were still sinners, Christ died for us" (Rom. 5:8). When Jesus was crucified to death on a cross and his blood spilled, he provided the "once for all" sacrifice so that blood sacrifices would no longer be necessary (Heb. 7:27). The blood of Jesus as the means of providing freedom from our sin (i.e., atonement) has its origin in the law of Moses.

The Mosaic law was given by God to the nation of Israel (Exod. 19; Rom. 9:4) with the purpose of setting apart Israel from other nations, revealing the character of God and the sinfulness of human beings, and demonstrating that only Christ could fulfill the law. The law of Moses consisted of three parts: the Ten Commandments, the way of worship, and the ordinances. It stated that once a year the Jewish priest was to make an offering of the blood of animals on the altar of the temple for the sins of the people. The offering of the blood of animals was required as a cleansing for sin, without which there would be no forgiveness (Heb. 9:22). It was believed that life was in the blood; the giving of life was required as an offering for the forgiveness of sin. Jesus's blood, as a nineteenth-century hymn stated, covers our sin so that God will pardon us. The promise of God's forgiveness gives us hope and peace:

> What can wash away my sin?
> Nothing but the blood of Jesus;

What can make me whole again?
Nothing by the blood of Jesus.

Oh! Precious is the flow
That makes me white as snow;
No other fount I know,
Nothing but the blood of Jesus.

For my pardon, this I see,
Nothing but the blood of Jesus;
For my cleansing this my plea,
Nothing but the blood of Jesus.

Nothing can for sin atone,
Nothing but the blood of Jesus;
Naught of good that I have done,
Nothing but the blood of Jesus.

This is all my hope and peace,
Nothing but the blood of Jesus;
This is all my righteousness,
Nothing but the blood of Jesus.[12]

Jesus Christ takes on all of the brokenness of the world, thus restoring the world to wholeness and beauty. He, who is God's self-disclosure, comes to renew the world and restore God's people. We can be rescued, not to live dispassionate, otherworldly lives but rather to be driven more deeply into the world to be instruments of God's goodness and reconciliation wherever there is brokenness.

What is so distinct about the metanarrative of God with us in Jesus Christ is that through Jesus God demonstrates what has been famously called "amazing grace." It is amazing because God shows us mercy not because of anything we have accomplished but entirely because of God's love and goodness. It is amazing because no matter how far "off the mark" we are, God's grace is sufficient to overcome: "But where sin increased, grace increased all the more" (Rom. 5:20). Grace is often defined as God's "unmerited favor" and "loving-kindness," since God extends God's love and forgiveness to us. Those who accept Christ's death and resurrection as a covering

12. Robert Lowry, "Nothing but the Blood," 1876 (public domain).

for their sins live "under grace" (Rom. 6:15). Our human proclivity is to live according to the law, our own accomplishments and efforts, but we will have peace with God only if we live by God's grace (John 1:17; Eph. 2:8–10).

*Act 4: God restores.* The grand narrative of the Bible does not end with redemption since God has promised renewal of the whole world. The Bible states that all of creation will be restored, like a new birth, with a new heaven and a new earth. The old creation will not be tossed away but will be renewed, not in an otherworldly sense but as an earth that is a new creation (Rev. 21:1). God will restore creation, not obliterate it. Everything that God made, which is true and beautiful, will be set free from all sorrow and pain: "The desert and the parched land will be glad; the wilderness will rejoice and blossom" (Isa. 35:1). The good news of the gospel is that this new creation has already begun with the death and resurrection of Jesus Christ. This fact gives Christians reason to celebrate.

## The Translated Word

That Jesus was God incarnate is a marvelous demonstration of God's intention of translating his love for us in the most meaningful way, by being clothed in human skin and culture. Jesus was a Jew. Andrew Walls states succinctly, "Any confidence we have in the translatability of the Bible rests on that prior act of translation. There is a history of translation of the Bible because there is a translation of the Word into flesh."[13] Yet God's intention was not to promote one culture over another, the Jews over the gentiles, or gentiles over the Jews. Ethnicity is relativized in the light of the revelation of Christ.

Christianity is the most culturally and linguistically diverse religion, a testimony to what is fundamental to its distinctive character as a faith tradition. Neither Christ nor the church universal required that believers learn a new language in order to be a Christian. Even when Hebrew, Latin, or Greek were major languages of the

13. Andrew F. Walls, *The Missionary Movement in Christian History: Studies in the Transmission of Faith* (Maryknoll, NY: Orbis, 1996), 26.

church in worship, Christians could and did pray in their vernacular languages.

Christianity is a movement of translation, geared toward communicating God's Word in local languages in order to convey effectively the meaning of the Bible to all people. Yet translation was a costly endeavor. For example, John Wycliffe (ca. 1330–84) and William Tyndale (1494–1536) were martyred because of their efforts to translate the Bible into vernacular languages. The resistance to Bible translation was uneven throughout the history of the church, with the sixteenth century being the deadliest period for Bible translators. In some areas of the world today, Bible translators are still targeted and murdered for their work.

The translated word gave rise to massive social transformation worldwide. One of South Africa's preeminent social scientists, Monica Wilson, observed that Christianity in South Africa did not stop at proclaiming the power of God but went on to demand a fundamental transformation of the way of life of their converts, which had dramatic social and cultural consequences. That Jesus had the power to cure people afflicted by spirits, feed the hungry, and heal the blind had immense social and political implications. Policy analyst Ann Bernstein summarizes Wilson's insights about South African converts, underscoring not only the social impact of the translated Bible but also the dilemma of converts vis-à-vis their traditional ways of life.

> These converts were the radicals within African societies—the individuals ready to embrace change. Others castigated them as collaborators and colonial stooges. Notwithstanding this, it was these groups of converts who provided the basis for the development of an educated African elite that dominated leadership positions within African society in the twentieth century. Their experience of alienation and exclusion with the colonial order persuaded some to attempt to rebuild their connections with traditional society, but these attempts were made across the considerable cultural chasm that their initial immersion in missionary Christianity had opened up between them and their societies of origin.[14]

14. Ann Bernstein, "Can South Africa Be More Than an Offshoot of the West?," in *Many Globalizations: Cultural Diversity in the Contemporary World*, ed. Peter L. Berger and Samuel P. Huntington (New York: Oxford University Press, 2003), 193.

Yale historian Lamin Sanneh states that the vast majority of African independence movements on the continent were led by men raised in missionary Bible schools, where they read God's Word in their local language and learned that they too bore the image of God and, therefore, refused to be dominated by colonial overlords. Bible translation often gave rise to cultural revitalization as readers learned about a God who created the world, loved them, and invited them to be children of God. That shift in ultimate authority served to threaten the prevailing powers.

Why would the word—and reading—be such a threat? It is difficult for us today to imagine the power of words in a world in which literacy was considered a threat. Regarding the slave revolt in Bahia, Brazil, in 1835, anthropologist Jack Goody wrote, "So worried did the authorities become about the power of the book in the hands of the slaves that those who could read and write were packed off back to West Africa, leaving behind the illiterates, who were less likely to engage in an effective struggle."[15] Being literate empowers individuals and communities. "Illiteracy is the means by which the powerful control the powerless to maintain their dominion."[16]

It is important to keep in mind a simple fact often overlooked by scholars investigating the consequences of Bible translation: Bible translation is done by Bible translators. Too frequently discussions of the impact of Bible translation focus on such themes as cultural renewal, the role of the Holy Spirit, and the personal transformation of converts. Less attention is given to the translators themselves as embodying Christianity and conveying in their very presence, material goods, attitudes, preferences, and values the practices of the faith.

## The Bible in Context

The Bible was written in specific contexts. Likewise, it is interpreted in a variety of contexts. When interpreting the Bible, individuals and

15. Jack Goody, *The Power of the Written Tradition* (Washington: Smithsonian Institution Press, 2000), 164–65.
16. Don Edwards, *Is Hearing Enough? Literacy and the Great Commandments* (Pasadena, CA: William Carey Library, 2010), 4.

communities make sense of it through their own perspectives, along with the questions and needs of their particular contexts. Since the twentieth century, interpretations of the Bible range from fundamentalist perspectives of inerrancy (the Bible being without error, including in matters of science, geography, and history) to heavily critical ones where the Bible loses its authority entirely—or at most is seen as just one authority among other sources of knowledge. These approaches give shape to particular forms of Christianity. While it is impossible to do justice to the immense variety of contexts in which the Bible is engaged, here are a few core samplings of contemporary biblical interpretative strategies.

It is said that the church in Africa emphasizes healing, vision, and power—all themes within the Bible. The African Independent Churches (AIC), the most dynamic churches on the continent, are marked by their spirit-led worship. When confronting a woman who believed herself to be possessed by an evil spirit during a prayer service, Zambian archbishop Emmanuel Milingo recognized—when all medical and psychiatric help failed—that the woman had been overpowered by the Holy Spirit and was healed. After this event, Archbishop Milingo dedicated his ministry to healing activities that he understood to be based on the authority of the Bible. Yet his view of healing, founded on his reading of the Bible, entailed liberation in many parts of Africa from all forms of oppression, both spiritual and material, throughout the continent.[17]

In general, African Christians do not separate the Bible from other forms of knowledge. According to African studies professor Gerrie ter Haar, "The Bible remains the most important spiritual *and* intellectual resource for African Christians."[18] The place of the Bible in the lives of African Christians distinguishes them from Western Christians. Ter Haar notes that immigrant African Christians in Europe carry their Bible with them, and from the Bible they critique European society around them, couched in a spirit idiom. In Africa, and among African diasporic Christians, the material and the spiritual worlds are interconnected, the visible and the invisible overlap.

17. See Gerrie ter Haar, *How God Became African: African Spirituality and Western Secular Thought* (Philadelphia: University of Pennsylvania Press, 2009), 4–5.
18. Ter Haar, *How God Became African*, 97.

Asian American biblical hermeneutics provides insights that can enliven our understanding and shift our orientation. Tat-Siong Benny Liew researches the intersection of Asian American biblical hermeneutics and postcolonial theory. His thesis seeks to challenge both nationalism and imperialism. Liew argues for the concept of "yin-yang eyes" in his biblical hermeneutics, aiming to explore the oppressive as well as liberating potential of the Bible. From another Asian perspective, writings of R. S. Sugirtharajah, a Sri Lankan emeritus biblical scholar at the University of Birmingham, explore Bible interpretation from the so-called Third World (i.e., the Majority World), highlighting themes of postcolonial biblical criticism, the Asian faces of Jesus, and themes at the intersection of Bible and empire. Sugirtharajah examines overlooked aspects of biblical texts marshaled by Victorian preachers to strengthen British imperial intentions in South Asia, thus illustrating the power of postcolonial interpretations and the use of the Bible among colonizers and the subjugated.

Latin America is said to be the birthplace of liberation theology, where theologians Gustavo Gutiérrez (Peru), Leonardo Boff (Brazil), Jon Sobrino (Spain), and Juan Luis Segundo (Uruguay) promoted the phrase "preferential option for the poor," in which they employed a combination of elements of Marxist social analysis and biblical hermeneutics with the aim of exposing systems of oppression of indigenous populations and liberating the subjugated from structural sin. Their biblical interpretation called for orthopraxis (right practice) against poverty and the sin behind all systems of oppression, based on their biblical interpretation.[19] Latin American liberation theology inspired a similar reading of Scripture in a variety of contexts worldwide, influencing the development of black liberation theology (United States and worldwide), feminist theology (United States and worldwide), Dalit theology (India), Minjung theology (South Korea), and other forms of social action.

Polynesia, Micronesia, and Melanesia consist of thousands of islands comprising one of the most Christianized regions in the world. Pacific Island Christianity began in Polynesia, with the conversion of chiefs, and then moved westward into Micronesia and then

19. See, e.g., Isa. 61:1; Matt. 10:34; Luke 22:35–38.

finally into Melanesia. In large part due to the archipelagic nature of the Pacific nations, different island groups interpret the Bible through their own epistemological categories, often reconfiguring indigenous concepts along biblical lines. For instance, in Melanesia and Polynesia, where *mana* has been for decades recognized by anthropologists as meaning supernatural force or power, in local translations of the Bible the term is used to mean "effective action," "miracle," "wonders," "mighty works," thus hastening a shift in the Pacific Islander understanding of the term. Earlier notions of *mana* underwent change as a new sense of *mana* was created via the Bible's translation into local idioms.[20] As in many other places around the world, particularly where the Bible was the first book to be translated into the local language, in Samoa and many other regions of the Pacific, the final form of the Bible set standards for written and spoken languages.[21]

Dreaming is a major feature of Pacific Islander religious life. It is said that many features of Pacific Islander worldviews originated in dreams. Although dreams are common in the Bible, mainline Protestant churches have mostly dismissed dreams in the region as being unscientific. Yet charismatic-pentecostal Pacific Island Christians connect well with dreaming as a source of knowledge.

North American and European biblical hermeneutics reflects similar challenges as other regions of the world, such as debates between those who hold a literal view of history or a figurative one. Young-earth creationists, who interpret Genesis 1 as saying that God created the world in six twenty-four-hour periods, contend against those who advocate for intelligent design or evolutionary creationism. What role does reason play in interpreting the Bible? How do the insights of science relate to knowledge of the world as presented in Scripture? North American biblical interpretation shares many of the same challenges as other regions of the world, but what seems unique to the region is the extent to which many biblical scholars seek scientific objectivity as a guide to that process.

20. Matt Tomlinson, "Mana: Bible Translation and Discourse of Loss in Fiji," *Oceania* 76, no. 2 (2006): 173–85.
21. See John Garrett, *To Live among the Stars: Christian Origins in Oceania* (Geneva: World Council of Churches, 1982), 126.

The Bible is meaningful to Christians because God speaks through its words, revealing the character of God, God's love for us, and our purpose as human beings. Through its words we receive comfort to endure times of suffering and guidance to make sense of our lives. God's Word gives us hope and helps us navigate life's difficulties. Through it we know that we are not alone. Together the church is shaped by Scripture to become ever more like the One who inspired its words.

An appropriate way to conclude this chapter on the Bible is with a statement about the Bible from Gideons International, known for providing Bibles and New Testaments around the world in more than ninety-five languages. Most of us know Gideons International from the Bibles they place in hotel bedside tables. They are placed there to provide comfort and hope to those in need, with these words printed inside.

> Read [the Bible] to be wise, believe it to be safe, and practice it to be holy. It contains light to direct you, food to support you, and comfort to cheer you.
>
> It is the traveler's map, the pilgrim's staff, the pilot's compass, the soldier's sword, and the Christian's charter. Here too, Heaven is opened and the gates of Hell disclosed.
>
> Christ is its grand subject, our good its design, and the glory of God its end. It should fill the memory, rule the heart, and guide the feet. Read it slowly, frequently and prayerfully. It is a mine of wealth, a paradise of glory, and a river of pleasure.
>
> It is given you in life, will be opened at the judgment, and be remembered forever. It involves the highest responsibility, rewards the greatest labor, and will condemn all who trifle with its sacred contents.[22]

22. "An Inspiring Introduction to the Holy Book," *The Gideons International* (blog), December 31, 2010, http://blog.gideons.org/2010/12/the-bible-contains-the -mind-of-god/.

# 4

# What Is the Christian Church?

O n the south coast of the western half of the island of New
Guinea, in a region once referred to as Irian Jaya but now
called West Papua, lies a massive thatched-roofed structure
that looks more like a round beehive than the typical church you
might see in New York, London, or Seoul. Gathered inside are clans
of Sawi, a tribal group with a history of clan warfare. The Sawi once
held treachery as their highest virtue; individuals would befriend
members of other Sawi clans and then, after gaining their confidence,
cannibalize them, celebrating their treacherous act through song and
dance while eating the flesh of their victim. For years the Sawi cycle
of befriending and betraying led to a history of distrust among clans.

In the early 1960s, Christian missionaries learned that the Sawi
had a rarely used tradition of peacemaking that could surprisingly
reestablish peace among warring clans. The peacemaking ritual required that a clan leader give his infant son to the leader of the enemy
clan. The Sawi called this son the Peace Child. As long as the child
survived, peace would be maintained between the warring clans. Once
the Peace Child died, peace was no longer guaranteed. When missionaries Don and Carol Richardson communicated that God gave
his only Son, Jesus Christ, as a once-and-for-all Peace Child, the Sawi
received that message with great enthusiasm, since the God-man,

Jesus Christ, would never die. Peace would be eternal. This message led to the mass conversion of the Sawi, where peace holds today and the Sawi church continues unabated. After becoming Christians, the Sawi worshiped in a beehive church. Former enemy clans now celebrate peace and common fellowship with one another, using cooked sago palm and water from an aluminum can for the body and blood of Jesus during the celebration of the Lord's Supper.[1]

Another church, located three thousand miles away from the Sawi church, is Yoido Full Gospel Church, in Seoul, South Korea, the world's largest church. With membership of half a million people, this Assemblies of God church, founded by Pastor David Yonggi Cho in 1958, is a massive Pentecostal congregation with a complex of church and administration buildings on Yoi island in the middle of the Han River. Today, the church is led by senior pastor Young Hoon Lee, with hundreds of pastors serving alongside him. Yoido Full Gospel Church has a 120-member white-robed choir, a full orchestra, and simultaneous translation into six languages. People in the congregation speak of experiencing the power of the Holy Spirit and being healed from sorrow, pain, and physical ailments. Worship is energetic, with people raising their hands in the air; preaching is charismatic, personally applicable, and accessible to a wide variety of people in the assembly. When the church doors open at 7:00 a.m. on Sunday, parishioners run down toward the front, to be closer to the power of healing. Despite the massive size of the main sanctuary, which contains bright lights and two huge screens flanking the massive cross in the center of the front of the sanctuary, the space is relatively simple and unadorned, without stained-glass windows.

We ought not make the mistake of thinking in evolutionary terms about the church around the world—for example, that the Sawi church represents a more primitive form of the Yoido church. Both are the church. The church worldwide is highly diverse, in part because it reflects the language, ethnicity, architecture, and ways of life of the local communities that make up those assemblies. Amidst all

---

1. The events of the Peace Child and work of missionaries Don and Carol Richardson are presented in Don Richardson, *Peace Child*, 4th ed. (Bloomington, MN: Bethany, 2005).

this diversity, it is important to recognize that the church is the body of Jesus Christ in the world as he was in the world.

In this chapter I focus on the identity of the church and leave the discussion of worship, which is a paramount expression of the church, for the next chapter. The nature of the Christian church has been a hotly debated topic throughout the history of the faith. What are its origins? How did it start? In this chapter I begin by suggesting that the church is something new—albeit with continuity with past Jewish experience of worship and belief. Second, I define the word "church" and give background on the ways the church is similar to and different from other institutions. Third, I present the church as both one and many, since amid its immense diversity in theology and worship style the church is essentially unified as the one body of Christ. Fourth, I underscore the fact that the church is not simply an inwardly looking organization; the church exists in its actions outside of itself. As such, we will see the dual function of the church as both gathering (i.e., worship) and sending (i.e., mission).

Fifth, I consider the basic teachings of the church. Regardless of the denomination, common subjects are taught throughout the church worldwide, even with various emphases on certain elements. Sixth, I suggest that a good definition of the church includes the celebration of the sacraments. Here I will introduce the various sacraments that give shape to the major branches of the church. Seventh, I answer the question, How does one understand a particular church (the church particular) within the context of so many churches (the church universal)? This section will discuss the differences within the church through the helpful insights from what has been called the Wesleyan Quadrilateral and from the church models presented by Avery Cardinal Dulles.

## Something New

In the disciples' last meeting with Jesus, after he had been resurrected from the dead, Jesus said, "You are witnesses of these things. I am going to send you what my Father has promised; but stay in the city until you have been clothed with power from on high" (Luke 24:48–49). Following that command, the disciples and others gathered in

an upper room of a house when, on the day of Pentecost, the Holy
Spirit descended on them, marking the beginning of the church.

> When the day of Pentecost came, they were all together in one place.
> Suddenly a sound like a blowing of a violent wind came from heaven
> and filled the whole house where they were sitting. They saw what
> seemed to be tongues of fire that separated and came to rest on each
> of them. All of them were filled with the Holy Spirit and began to
> speak in other tongues as the Spirit enabled them.
>
> Now there were staying in Jerusalem God-fearing Jews from every
> nation under heaven. When they heard this sound, a crowd came to-
> gether in bewilderment, because each one heard their own language
> being spoken. Utterly amazed, they asked: "Aren't all these who are
> speaking Galileans? Then how is it that each of us hears them in our
> native language? Parthians, Medes and Elamites; residents of Meso-
> potamia, Judea and Cappadocia, Pontus and Asia, Phrygia and Pam-
> phylia, Egypt and the parts of Libya near Cyrene; visitors from Rome
> (both Jews and converts to Judaism); Cretans and Arabs—we hear
> them declaring the wonders of God in our own tongues!" Amazed
> and perplexed, they asked one another, "What does this mean?" . . .
>
> Then Peter stood up with the Eleven, raised his voice and addressed
> the crowd: "Fellow Jews and all of you who live in Jerusalem, let me
> explain this to you; listen carefully to what I say. . . .
>
> "Therefore let all Israel be assured of this: God has made this Jesus,
> whom you crucified, both Lord and Messiah."
>
> When the people heard this, they were cut to the heart and said to
> Peter and the other apostles, "Brothers, what shall we do?"
>
> Peter replied, "Repent and be baptized, every one of you, in the name
> of Jesus Christ for the forgiveness of your sins. And you will receive
> the gift of the Holy Spirit. The promise is for you and your children
> and for all who are far off—for all whom the Lord our God will call."
>
> . . . Those who accepted his message were baptized, and about
> three thousand were added to their number that day. (Acts 2:1–12,
> 14, 36–39, 41)

The church began with the descent of tongues of fire, which filled
people with the Holy Spirit. Immediately following this powerful
event, the group that was filled with the Holy Spirit "devoted themselves to the apostles' teaching and to fellowship, to the breaking of

bread and to prayer. Everyone was filled with awe at the many wonders and signs performed by the apostles. . . . And the Lord added to their number daily those who were being saved" (Acts 2:42–43, 47).

The apostolic mission entailed the sending of apostles throughout the world to share the message of repentance, forgiveness, and peace with God through Jesus Christ. After Pentecost, Christianity became centrifugal, moving out of its place of origin to the ends of the earth.

Yet we need to reach back further than the events of Acts 2 to understand the meaning and significance of the church. The meaning of the church is connected to a theological affirmation about the Triune God. The love within the Godhead, which reflects God's nature and character, spills forth through God's creative actions. God has sent the church for the purpose of being the sign and instrument of God's kingdom throughout the world. The church exists because of the mission of God (Latin *missio Dei*). The *missio Dei* refers to God the Father sending the Son, who sends the Holy Spirit, who sends the church. God is a sending God: God the Father, sending God the Son, sending God the Holy Spirit. The *missio Dei* was a sixteenth-century Jesuit concept used to express the nature of the church in the world. Without mission, the church would not be the church. The church exists because of mission, not the reverse.

Therefore, it is important to recognize that the church is not just an institution, as a sociological entity, but rather is grounded in and sustained by the sending of God. In the words of Lesslie Newbigin, "The truth is that the church is not the church in any New Testament sense unless it *is* a mission. . . . I very much like the phrase of Emil Brunner 'the church exists by mission as fire exists by burning.' . . . By detaching mission from the church we have grievously corrupted in practice the whole conception of what the Church is."[2]

## The Assembly of God

Biblical scholars note that the early church's use of the term *ekklēsia* to mean "church" must have been anachronistic and fraught with

2. Lesslie Newbigin, *The Household of God: Lectures on the Nature of the Church* (New York: Friendship, 1954), 142.

confusion to the ordinary Greek of the day, since Christians used *ekklēsia* in a peculiar way.[3] Prior to the emergence of Christianity, *ekklēsia* referred to a town meeting of free male Roman citizens. Wayne Meeks states that this definition of *ekklēsia* as a voluntary meeting of Roman citizens "continued to be so employed even though the Hellenistic and then the Roman monarchies had robbed the voting assemblies of much of their power."[4]

*Ekklēsia* comes from a verb meaning "to call out," with the implication that those called out form a congregation, assembly, gathering, or council for discussing and deciding public business.[5] As I mentioned in chapter 1, nothing is Christian at the start. Rather, one *becomes* Christian: "Lord," "baptism," and "church" were pre-Christian ideas and practices that became Christian in the light of the revelation of Jesus Christ. Likewise, Christians did not invent the notion of *ekklēsia*.

Furthermore, in ancient Greece an *ekklēsiastērion*, a theater or place of popular assembly, was a specific building for the purpose of holding the meetings of the *ekklēsia* in a democratic Greek city-state. Although there were only a few cities in antiquity that had *ekklēsiastēria* of their own, these spaces were connected to financial transactions. For instance, in the currency decree from ancient Oblia in the region of Sardinia, Italy, currency exchanges had to take place on the stone of the *ekklēsiastērion*; the exchange could not take place anywhere else, or the seller or buyer would be punished.[6] However, there was a distinction between *ekklēsia* and *ekklēsiastērion*: "*Ekklēsia* is the gathering of saints, assembled together by means of the right faith and an excellent way of life, while *ekklēsiastērion* is just the church building. The former is composed of unblemished souls, the latter is built of stone and wood."[7]

3. Wayne A. Meeks, *The First Urban Christians: The Social World of the Apostle Paul* (New Haven: Yale University Press, 1983), 108.

4. Meeks, *First Urban Christians*, 108.

5. See J. C. Lambert, "Chose; Chosen," in *International Standard Bible Encyclopedia*, ed. James Orr, 5 vols. (Grand Rapids: Eerdmans, 1929), 1:651.

6. Alain Bresson, *The Making of the Ancient Greek Economy: Institutions, Markets, and Growth in the City-States*, trans. Steven Rendall (Princeton, NJ: Princeton University Press, 2016), 507n73.

7. Gerasimos Merianos and George Gotsis, *Managing Financial Resources in Late Antiquity: Greek Fathers' Views on Hoarding and Saving*, New Approaches to Byzantine History and Culture (London: Palgrave Macmillan, 2018), 125.

Christians, who were not always "free male Roman citizens" of the empire, adopted the term *ekklēsia* and applied it to their own assemblies. The meetings were peculiar because they were not called together by one another or by powers of the state. Rather, they were called together by God. *Ekklēsia theou*, "the assembly of God," conveyed the conviction that God was the leader of these assemblies. The Christian church, the assembly of God, was instituted for the purpose of being the sign and instrument of the kingdom of God.

In the Greek translation of the Old Testament, *ekklēsia* was used for the assemblies of Israel when they gathered before the Lord for religious purposes, for they were "called out" from the nations to be God's special people (Rom. 9:4). In the New Testament, *ekklēsia* referred not only to an occasional meeting but also to the group itself.

Paul adopts *ekklēsia* in his letters—for instance, when he addresses "the *ekklēsia* of the Thessalonians" (1 Thess. 1:1; 2 Thess. 1:1), or when the people in a town come together in *ekklēsia* (1 Cor. 11:18). Paul uses *ekklēsia* in the plural (*ekklēsiai*), such as "all the *ekklēsiai* of Christ" (Rom. 16:16), but also in the singular to speak of the entire Christian movement—for example, "the *ekklēsia* of God" (1 Cor. 10:32), referring to, in Meeks's words, a "formal gathering of all the tribes of ancient Israel or their representatives."[8] *Ekklēsia* refers to both small and large assemblies of God's people, as well as the universal people of God worldwide. It is instructive to note that the encouragement for one assembly to remember another gathering elsewhere (e.g., "the *ekklēsiai* of Asia greet you" [1 Cor. 16: 19]) also represents the expression of the larger, universal fellowship of the assembly (1 Cor. 1:2; 16:19–21; 2 Cor. 1:1).

After we learn what the church is—a meeting called by God—we have to ask follow-up questions: Who goes to church? Are all those who go to church Christian? Does one have to be Christian to go to church? Can we assume that all who identify themselves as Christians and go to church are without fault?

For Augustine, the church included both sinner and saint. Robert Louis Wilken notes Augustine's view: "chaff among the wheat, men and women who were manifestly not holy but who as members of

8. Meeks, *First Urban Christians*, 108.

the Church were in the process of being healed."[9] Augustine claimed
that sinners were not justified currently but were being made just;
the "line between devout believers and those who went through the
motions of believing was so faint as to be invisible."[10] Augustine's
perspective contrasted sharply with the Donatists, who argued that
the church was a body of saints only within which sinners had no
place, thus erecting a stark boundary between the church and the
world, saint and sinner. Augustine argued for the unity of the church,
"a 'mixed body' of saints and sinners, refusing to weed out those
who had lapsed under persecution or for other reasons."[11] Indeed,
in every congregation there are people who are Christians and those
who are not but attend for a variety of reasons (e.g., the aesthetics
of the service, the music and moral teaching, civic or family duty).

## How Many Churches Are There Today?

There is one church, one body of Christ. That one church finds its
existence in particular churches. One church consisting of many
churches means that Christians from one part of the world can worship freely with other Christians from vastly different geographic
regions, even though their churches might be dissimilar.

There are many different kinds of Christian churches, each with
distinctive emphases regarding worship, authority, and theology, yet
all with the same foundational affirmations. All churches affirm that
God is triune, consisting of Father, Son, and Holy Spirit, sharing
the same essence; God the Son was sent to save human beings from
death and sin by dying on the cross and being raised again; there is
an end to time when all people will be judged by God; reconciliation
with God comes only through the payment that Jesus made on the
cross by shedding his blood on our behalf; the church is the body of
Christ on earth, where Christians are nurtured and sent out to share

9. Robert Louis Wilken, *The First Thousand Years: A Global History of Christianity* (New Haven: Yale University Press), 187.
10. Wilken, *First Thousand Years*, 187.
11. Alister McGrath, *Christian Theology: An Introduction* (Oxford: Blackwell,
1994), 20.

in word and deed the good news that God loves us and we can be forgiven and have peace with God.

How many churches are there in the world? A typical way to categorize the various branches of the church within the one universal church is to use four groups: Roman Catholic, Protestant (including Anglicans), Orthodox, and Independents. "Independents" refers to African Initiated Churches, Chinese house churches, the Vineyard, and other Christian churches that are a mutually exclusive tradition apart from Catholic, Orthodox, and Protestant.

| | DENOMINATIONS | | CONGREGATIONS | |
| --- | --- | --- | --- | --- |
| | Total | Average size | Total | Average size |
| Catholics | 234 | 405,000 | 280,000 | 4,280 |
| Orthodox | 11,340 | 249,000 | 130,500 | 2,160 |
| Protestants | 11,330 | 48,000 | 1,740,000 | 310 |
| Independents | 31,600 | 13,000 | 2,955,000 | 140 |
| **Total** | **44,294** | 52,000 | **5,105,500** | 480 |

Source: Todd M. Johnson and Gina A. Zurlo, eds., *World Christian Database* (Leiden/Boston: Brill, accessed April 2018).

In 2015, there were approximately 44,000 Christian denominations and 5.1 million congregations in the world. Non-Christians might wonder in bewilderment, "What religion are you, Methodist or Catholic?" Catholics will usually self-ascribe as "Catholic," yet refer to other Christians as "Christian." Yet Catholics are Christian. And Christians are all "catholic," in that they are a part of the one universal church.

We can learn much about the diverse nature of the church from early Christians. Early believers in Ephesus, for instance, recognized that there was one congregation: "There is one body and one Spirit, just as you were called to one hope when you were called; one Lord, one faith, one baptism; one God and Father of all, who is over all and through all and in all" (Eph. 4:4–6). Yet evidence in Corinth shows that early believers were divided: "I appeal to you, brothers and sisters, in the name of our Lord Jesus Christ, that all of you agree with one another in what you say and that there be no divisions among you, but that you be perfectly united in mind and thought. My brothers and sisters, some from Chloe's household have informed me that there are quarrels among you. What I mean is this: One of you says, 'I follow Paul'; another, 'I follow Apollos'; another, 'I follow Cephas'; still another, 'I follow Christ.' Is Christ divided?" (1 Cor. 1:10–13). Paul bemoaned the divisions in the early church (1 Cor. 11:18); nevertheless, it did not take long for divisions to develop and threaten the unity of the church.

Many divisions resulted from heresy. The term "heresy" (*hairesis*) comes from a Greek word that originally meant "choice" or "thing chosen." Early heresy in the church meant choosing for oneself rather than following church tradition. Heretics were those who followed a self-chosen, personal opinion that was distinct from the theological affirmations decided by the early church.

Some of the major heresies that were confronted by the church were (1) simony, named after Simon Magus, a magician in the New Testament who offered money to the apostles to tempt them to share their power with him, was the belief that spiritual goods can be bought or sold (see Acts 8:9–24) to gain church privileges such as pardons or forgiveness; (2) docetism, which denied Jesus's humanity, teaching that Jesus only appeared to be a man (Greek, *dokeō*, "to seem") (1 John 4:2–3; 2 John 1:7–11); and (3) Gnosticism, which emphasized esoteric "knowledge" (Greek *gnōsis*) over faith in and love for Christ (see 1 Cor. 8:1–3), argued that salvation was gained by quasi-intuitive knowledge of the mysteries of the universe rather than by faith in the human-divine Christ alone. Church divisions also occurred throughout the history of the church less for reasons of heresies but often because of different theological emphases and cultural and personal issues.

Since the twentieth century, ecumenical movements have sought to demonstrate unity within the Christian church. The main ecumenical bodies consist of the World Council of Churches and the Lausanne Movement. The World Council of Churches (WCC), founded in 1948, consists of 348 mostly mainline Protestant denominations, in more than 110 countries, and over 500 million Christians, including most of the world's Eastern Orthodox churches. The WCC promotes common witness in mission and evangelism (e.g., servicing human needs) and demonstrates the visible unity of the church. Headquartered in Geneva, Switzerland, the WCC is structured with regional (e.g., Middle East Council of Churches) and national (e.g., Communion of Churches in Indonesia) branches, making it a worldwide movement with local representation.

The Lausanne Movement represents evangelical denominations in more than 150 nations. Based in Lausanne, Switzerland, the Lausanne Movement, started in part by Billy Graham in 1974 and later led by John Stott, provides fellowship and witness, connecting leaders across the world to work collaboratively and prayerfully to communicate the gospel. With a strong emphasis on Christian mission, the Lausanne Movement seeks to engage in Christian ministry holistically across cultural and linguistic boundaries.

The Roman Catholic Church is the largest single church in Christianity. One of the major concerns of the Vatican II Council meeting (1962–65) was the restoration of unity among all Christians, exhorting all Catholics to participate in the work of Christian unity based on the Holy Spirit.

## The Body in Action

The church is a peculiar institution; it is both visible and invisible, material and spiritual. The assembly of God (*ekklēsia theou*), we recall, is not simply a meeting like other gatherings, such as Habitat for Humanity, the Rotary Club, or the Audubon Society. The church is primarily an assembly that worships together, is built up through encouragement and teaching, and is sent out—it is an apostolic congregation because it is called and sent by God to reach those outside it. Archbishop William Temple exclaimed that the church is the only society in the world that exists for the sake of those who are not members of it. Dietrich Bonhoeffer wrote, "The church is the church only when it exists for others. . . . The church must share in the secular problems of ordinary human life, not dominating, but helping and serving."[12] Furthermore, suggested Bonhoeffer, "The church must

12. Quoted in David Bosch, *Transforming Mission: Paradigm Shifts in Theology of Mission* (Maryknoll, NY: Orbis, 2011), 384.

not seek its own self-preservation but be 'open to the world' and in solidarity with others, especially the oppressed and suffering."[13] Orlando Costas stated succinctly, "The church is basically a missionary community, i.e., that her fundamental character can only be understood from the perspective of God's mission to the world. . . . The church is a miraculous redemptive community."[14]

Christians have been referred to as the pilgrim people, those who are spiritually nourished when gathered but whose living is directed, in Costas's words, "outside the camp." As such, Christians are to travel lightly (Matt. 10) since they are resident aliens (1 Pet. 2:11).[15] N. T. Wright compares the church to a river: "Like a river, they [people of all ethnicities and languages] all started in different places, but they have now brought their different streams into a single flow. . . . Though the church consists by definition of people from the widest possible variety of backgrounds, part of the point of it all is that they belong to one another, and are meant to be part of the same powerful flow, going now in the same single direction. Diversity gives way to unity."[16] Yet, Wright continues, that unity also gives rise to diversity, like branches of a plant that have been set off in all directions, with "some pointing almost directly upward, some reaching down to earth, some heading out over neighboring walls." He continues, "You'd hardly know that they were all from the same stem."[17] Furthermore, the church is an eschatological community, so that it is not satisfied just with the here and now but rather is geared toward the future, as a witness to hope in the eternal glory of Jesus Christ (1 Pet. 5:10–11).

The church's work involves actions both inside and outside of its assembly. Inside, the church teaches; shares fellowship, encouragement, and admonition; and celebrates the sacraments. The New Testament

13. Dietrich Bonhoeffer, *Letters and Papers from Prison*, trans. Isabel Best et al., ed. John W. de Gruchy (Minneapolis: Fortress, 2010), 26.

14. Orlando E. Costas, *The Church and Its Mission: A Shattering Critique from the Third World* (Wheaton: Tyndale, 1974), 8.

15. A popular rendering of this concept can be found in Stanley Hauerwas and William H. Willimon, *Resident Aliens: Life in the Christian Colony* (Nashville: Abingdon, 1989).

16. N. T. Wright, *Simply Christian: Why Christianity Makes Sense* (New York: HarperOne, 2006), 200.

17. Wright, *Simply Christian*, 200.

states clearly the scope and content of Christian teaching: "to grasp how wide and long and high and deep is the love of Christ, and to know this love that surpasses knowledge—that you may be filled to the measure of all the fullness of God" (Eph. 3:18b–19). The aim, then, of Christian teaching is not just knowledge about God, creation, and redemption, but action, to love God and others (1 Cor. 8:1b).

## Teachings

The content of Christian teaching varies among the churches, but all Christian churches seek wisdom from the Bible. Topics include the nature of God, the nature of the church, history, humanity, final judgment, sacraments, wisdom, heaven, hell, earth, baptism, prayer, salvation, sexuality, cosmology, psychology, culture, society, politics, doctrine, and countless others. In general, the formal teaching of the church is of at least three kinds: creeds, confessions, and catechisms. Weekly teaching occurs within the sermon or homily as a part of worship, with a huge variety of styles across the church worldwide.

Creeds are the basic beliefs, or rules of faith, that early church leaders, including the apostles, handed down through the generations to teach new believers the Christian faith. The creeds are drawn from the Bible. The earliest Christian creed is the remarkably simple statement "Jesus is Lord" (Rom. 10:9; 1 Cor. 12:3). Other New Testament creeds include, for instance, "For there is one God and one mediator between God and mankind, the man Christ Jesus" (1 Tim. 2:5). Another refers to Jesus:

> Who being in very nature God,
>> did not consider equality with God something to be used
>> to his own advantage;
> rather, he made himself nothing
>> by taking the very nature of a servant,
>> being made in human likeness.
> And being found in appearance as a man,
>> he humbled himself
>> by becoming obedient to death—
>> even death on a cross!

> Therefore God exalted him to the highest place
> and gave him the name that is above every name,
> that at the name of Jesus every knee should bow,
> in heaven and on earth and under the earth,
> and every tongue acknowledge that Jesus Christ is Lord,
> to the glory of God the Father. (Phil. 2:6–11)

The most enduring Christian creeds are the Apostles' Creed, Nicene Creed, Chalcedonian Creed, and Athanasian Creed.

Confessions set boundaries of faith that separate Christian faith from non-Christian traditions, and usually are more extensive than creeds. While confessions affirm the basic beliefs of Christianity, they focus on secondary topics within Christian living, such as the Lord's Supper, baptism, relationships with government, and predestination. All major Christian churches have confessions. For instance, the Lutherans use the Formula of Concord (1577), the Reformed use the Belgic Confession (1561), and Methodists affirm the Twenty-Five Articles of Religion (1784).

Catechisms are the teachings of the church that offer practical and more accessible guidance for Christian living. Although there are some differences within the church worldwide, the essential teachings are commonly accepted and recorded in the formal catechisms. For instance, the Catechism of the Catholic Church states, "In revealing his mysterious name, YHWH ('I AM WHO AM' or 'I AM WHO I AM'), God says who he is and by what name he is to be called."[18] The catechism can also be structured in the form of question and answer, such as the Heidelberg Catechism:

> Question: What do you believe when you say, "I believe in God, the Father almighty, creator of heaven and earth"?
> Answer: That the eternal Father of our Lord Jesus Christ, who out of nothing created heaven and earth and everything in them, who still upholds and rules them by his eternal counsel and providence, is my God and Father because of Christ the Son.[19]

18. Catholic Church, *The Catechism of the Catholic Church* (New York: Doubleday, 1995), 63.

19. The Reformed Church in the United States, *Heidelberg Catechism* (Nashville: Nelson, 2013), 35 (Q&A 26).

Likewise, the Lutheran (ELCA) Small Catechism has served as a basic instruction book and content for teaching for Lutherans. It is structured by statement and explication—for instance, "The First Commandment: You shall have no other gods. What does this mean? We should fear, love, and trust in God above all things."[20] All Christian churches, with or without a formal catechism, affirm this basic statement about God. The Westminster Shorter Catechism (1647) also uses a question-and-answer format, calling master (or leader) and student (or congregation) to participate. For example, it asks, "What is the chief end of man?" and then supplies the answer, "To glorify God and enjoy Him forever!" (Q&A 1).

These teachings of the church are meant to encourage intellectual and spiritual renewal through a comprehensive presentation of the essentials of the Christian faith. While immensely important for the church, neither catechisms nor creeds are considered sacred writing but rather are useful for clarifying the Bible, the life of Jesus Christ, and God's will for our lives.

Fellowship is another feature of what happens inside the church. Christian fellowship is a partnership to the mutual benefit of those in the congregation. Christian fellowship is unique because it entails reciprocity based on God's grace and unity in the Holy Spirit. The ontological reality of the congregation's existence within the life of the Triune God is the basis for Christian fellowship: "We proclaim to you what we have seen and heard, so that you also may have fellowship with us. And our fellowship is with the Father and with his Son, Jesus Christ" (1 John 1:3).[21]

A unique feature of life inside the church is the encouragement and admonition among members of the congregation. One of the ways that the Holy Spirit is made manifest in the congregation is through words of reassurance when the brokenness of the world, our communities, and ourselves overwhelms us. Christian encouragement is similar to other forms of encouragement because it provides support and hope. Yet Christian encouragement is also unique since it is a

20. Evangelical Lutheran Synod, *Luther's Small Catechism* (St. Louis: Concordia, 2017), 13.
21. See also John 17:20–21; Acts 2:42; 4:32; 1 Cor. 1:9; 2 Cor. 13:14; 1 John 1:7.

grace-filled reminder that lifts our hearts toward the Lord (Col. 4:8). Encouragement and admonishment are often mentioned together in the Bible as mutual ministries: "And we urge you, brothers and sisters, warn those who are idle and disruptive, encourage the disheartened, help the weak, be patient with everyone. . . . Do not quench the Spirit. Do not treat prophets with contempt but test them all; hold on to what is good, reject every kind of evil" (1 Thess. 5:14, 19–22).

You might be surprised to see the joining of encouragement, admonishment, and Holy Spirit in the previous verse. The Greek verb *parakaleō* appears throughout the New Testament to mean "urge, exhort, entreat, console, encourage, strengthen, comfort, instruct" (e.g., Acts 2:40; Heb. 3:13). A noun derived from the verb *parakaleō* is *paraklētos* ("comforter"), the word that Jesus used to refer to God the Holy Spirit (John 14–16). The Holy Spirit is the one who enacts and empowers all of these actions, so much so that to encourage and admonish Christian brothers and sisters allows the Holy Spirit to work in the life of both the encourager and the one being encouraged.

## Sacraments

A meaningful practice inside the Christian church is the celebration of the sacraments, the "heart of the expression of the church's faith."[22] The term "sacrament" is derived from the Latin *sacramentum*, "a consecrated thing or act," which is considered "something holy," a Latin translation of the Greek *mystērion* ("mystery"). Sacraments are the church's rituals or signs that Christians believe either convey or are symbolic of the unseen grace of God. God uses sacraments to communicate the love and mercy of God toward us not because of anything we have done to earn that grace. This grace is often referred to as sanctifying grace because it allows us to share in the life of the Triune God, which is remarkable. A sacrament is a visible form of God's grace.

22. Tremper Longman III, ed., *The Baker Illustrated Bible Dictionary* (Grand Rapids: Baker Books, 2013), 309.

According to Catholic tradition, sanctifying grace is the supernatural state of being infused by God, and it affects the whole soul, will, mind, and affections. It is sanctifying because it is a gift from God that makes one holy, enabling one to participate in the divine life. God's grace is both mediated and experienced through the sacraments of the churches.

Churches recognize a different number of sacraments. The Catholic Church recognizes seven sacraments: Baptism, Confirmation or Chrismation, Eucharist, Penance, Anointing of the Sick, Holy Orders, and Matrimony. The Orthodox Churches likewise affirm seven sacraments as the "major sacraments" but also consider anything that the church does as being sacramental. That is, Orthodox Churches do not limit the number of sacraments. Instead they use the term *mystēria* (i.e., holy mysteries) to refer to both the seven sacraments and everything in and of the Orthodox Church as sacramental or mystical. Most Protestant churches (e.g., Lutheran, Methodist, Reformed, evangelical) affirm just two sacraments: Baptism and Holy Communion (also known as the Lord's Supper).

Although the number of sacraments varies among Christian churches, most Christians worldwide value sacramental practices, even if not formally practiced. Given the theological breadth within the church worldwide, it is not surprising that the practice of celebrating the sacraments also reflects the unique qualities of the congregation. In the next chapter, on worship, I will give space to exploring this diversity. Nevertheless, all Christians are bound together by their participation in the sacraments, since all sacraments derive their authority not from the pastor or priest who administers the sacrament but from their centerpiece—Christ. In Augustine's words, "The word [Christ] must make the element a sacrament; otherwise, it remains an ordinary element."[23]

Life outside the church has countless opportunities for service, evangelism, and solidarity. As the church is in the world, it shares in the world's problems and seeks to be an instrument of justice and healing in broken places, on individual, communal, and structural

23. Kirsi I. Stjerna, *The Large Catechism of Dr. Martin Luther, 1529* (Minneapolis: Fortress, 2016), 404.

levels. Protestant theologian Orlando Costas's provocative declaration made fifty years ago rings true today as a description of the issue facing those North Atlantic congregations that have tended to isolate themselves from the wider world. The challenge, Costas writes, is "to be more integral in her view of mission because the non-affluent, poverty-stricken, exploited, and oppressed world is challenging Christianity (identified with the affluent world) to be consistent with the message she proclaims. . . . The issue today is not whether or not people are being converted to Christ but whether this is happening as part of a total process: is the church a community totally committed to and involved in the fulfillment of the gospel in the context of the concrete historical situations in which men and women find themselves?"[24]

Today, all branches of the church affirm the necessity of the gospel proclaimed in both word and deed. Since the 1970s, evangelicals have used the strongest language to affirm the gospel as one, rather than seeing a dichotomy between evangelism and social responsibility: "There is no biblical dichotomy between the word spoken and the word made visible in the lives of God's people. [People] will look as they listen and what they see must be at one with what they hear. . . . There are times when our communication may be by attitude and action only, and times when the spoken word will stand alone: but we must repudiate as demonic the attempt to drive a wedge between evangelism and social concern."[25]

Prior to this evangelical statement, the mainline Protestants of the World Council of Churches (Uppsala Assembly, 1968) noted the same: "A Christianity which has lost its vertical dimension has lost its salt and is not only insipid in itself, but useless to the world. But a Christianity which would use the vertical preoccupation as a means to escape from its responsibility for and in the common life of man is a denial of the incarnation."[26]

24. Costas, *The Church and Its Mission*, 11.
25. From the document *A Response to Lausanne*, quoted in Bosch, *Transforming Mission*, 416.
26. World Council of Churches, *The Uppsala Report 1968: Official Report of the Fourth Assembly of the World Council of Churches, Uppsala, July 4–20, 1968*, ed. Norman Goodall (Geneva: World Council of Churches, 1968), 318.

## What's the Difference?

The massive numbers of churches around the world can seem bewildering. How do we make sense of such an array of names and varieties and practices and beliefs? If we were to visit a dozen churches around the globe, we would most likely be confused if we did not know beforehand the common features that unite all churches. Here are a few helpful metaphors to envision differences in the church, from Protestant and Catholic perspectives.

First, the Wesleyan Quadrilateral was an attempt by Wesleyan theologians to organize the thinking of John Wesley (1703–93) on the different sources of knowledge in the church. Wesley's ideas, by the way, were adopted by Methodism, and the various church movements inspired by Methodist theology, such as several holiness churches (e.g., Global Wesleyan Alliance) as well as outgrowth movements such as the Brethren in Christ Church, Christian and Missionary Alliance, Free Methodist Church, and Nazarene Church. Although Wesley did not formulate the succinct statement that came to be known as the Wesleyan Quadrilateral, scholars of Wesley, such as Albert Outler, noted that Wesley believed there were four elements that must be taken in balance in the church: Scripture, tradition, reason, and experience. According to the United Methodist Church, "Wesley believed that the living core of the Christian faith was revealed in Scripture, illumined by tradition, vivified in personal experience, and confirmed by reason."[27] Scripture, however, is identified as primary, revealing the Word of God, for it contains all that is necessary for our salvation.

When we keep the Quadrilateral in mind, we see that all churches exhibit a combination of these four features, with each giving priority to one or another element. For Wesley, these four elements taken together brought maturity in a Christian's life. When applied to the church more broadly, they illuminate some of the emphases that make each church unique. For instance, Pentecostal churches emphasize the experience of the Holy Spirit, and Catholics emphasize tradition. These function as sources of knowledge for each church. And they help to give each a distinctive quality. You might be surprised

27. Charles Yrigoyen Jr., ed., *T&T Clark Companion to Methodism* (New York: T&T Clark, 2010), 420.

to learn, for instance, that there are more than two hundred million charismatic Catholics worldwide, that Protestants also take tradition seriously, and that Orthodox value experience. If you think of primary and secondary emphases, you will notice that all four categories are at play in every church.

A second way to understand church differences is provided by the Jesuit priest and theologian Avery Cardinal Dulles, whose useful metaphors illuminate the structure, authority, practices, and beliefs in the life of the church. Dulles's book *Models of the Church* is of great value for understanding the church worldwide (Catholic, Orthodox, Protestant). Dulles offers the following models of the church, arguing that the model of church as extending God's grace has special merit.

First, church as *institution* "defines the Church primarily in terms of its visible structures, especially the rights and powers of its officers."[28] The institutional view focuses on clerics (pope, pastors, bishops, priests) responsible for teaching (i.e., approved doctrines), sanctifying (i.e., administering sacraments), and ruling (i.e., governing faith and morals). Therefore, in this model, authority is vested in the ruling class—clerics and church officers—whose jurisdiction follows the pattern of the secular state. Dulles explains that the institutional model, which is public and visible, can be rigid and doctrinaire, and thus of all the models ought not be taken as primary.

Second, according to the model of the church as *mystical communion*, the church consists of human beings bound together by their participation in the Spirit of God through the living Christ. As such, the church is not institutional but communal, a spiritual and supernatural body in communion with the Triune God, expressed by the shared bonds of creed, worship, and fellowship. It is animated and sustained by the Holy Spirit.

Third, the church as *sacrament* means that the church is the visible manifestation of the grace of Christ in the human community. In this sense, the church as sacrament brings together features of the institutional and mystical communion. Here the church is seen as the communicator of God's grace in the world, as the presence of

28. Avery Cardinal Dulles, *Models of the Church* (New York: Image, 2002), 27.

God. A sacrament, says Dulles, is a socially constituted symbol of the presence of grace coming to fulfillment.[29]

Fourth, the church as *herald* refers to the church's emphasis on hearing the word of God, putting its faith in Jesus Christ as Lord and Savior, and proclaiming the gospel everywhere. This model prioritizes proclamation of the word, for the church heralds the message of the kingdom of God, calling the church and the world to renewal and reformation. Evangelism is primary.

Fifth, the church as *servant* underscores the reality that the church shares in the struggles and joys of the human community. The church announces the coming kingdom of God not only in word but also through its ministry of reconciliation, healing wounds, since, like Christ, the church demonstrates that it exists for others.

Sixth, the church as *community of disciples* is an amalgamation of the other five models, with the recognition that the pilgrim church always seeks to be renewed. Here the church is seen holistically as an assembly of people living a common life with one another and the Triune God. As such, the church itself becomes a witnessing community, an alternative to the world's values and patterns of living.

Most churches have a mixture of these six models, but one or two will be predominant. Generally, Catholics believe that God speaks through the Bible, the Catholic Church, and the pope, so tradition is prioritized. Both Catholic and Orthodox churches affirm apostolic succession—that is, the uninterrupted transmission of spiritual authority from the apostles through successive popes and bishops, as successors of the apostle Peter.

Protestants believe that God speaks through the Word (Bible) preached and the Holy Spirit to guide the church and individual believers. Pentecostals emphasize the experience and the manifestation of the power of the Holy Spirit through the gifts of the Spirit. Leaders of the Protestant Reformation, emerging at a time of Catholic abuse of power in the sixteenth century, distinguished their affirmations using five Latin *solas* ("alones") that would guide their understanding of God, the church, Christian living, and salvation. These were *sola scriptura* ("by Scripture alone"), *sola fide* ("by faith

---

29. Dulles, *Models of the Church*, 59.

alone"), *sola gratia* ("by grace alone"), *solus Christus* ("through Christ alone"), and *soli Deo gloria* ("glory to God alone").[30] The Catholic response, sanctioned by the Council of Trent (1545–63), made faith and good works coordinate sources of justification, with stress on works, whereas Protestants insisted on the priority of faith for salvation.

Today, the differences between Catholics and Protestants, while still present, have diminished significantly, "to a degree that might have shocked Christians in past centuries."[31] More Protestants report that they believe salvation comes through a mix of faith and good works: About half of Protestants in the United States (52 percent) say that both good deeds and faith in God are needed to attain salvation, a historically Catholic position. The other half (46 percent) say that faith alone is needed.[32]

## Coffeehouse Church?

Rather than go to church, why not enjoy time at a local coffeehouse, meet with like-minded Christian brothers and sisters, and read Scripture together? Is reading Scripture with Christian friends at the local coffeehouse the same as going to church? Even the "nones" of the Pew Research Center data—those who do not self-identify as followers of any religious tradition—might find reading scriptures (of any religion) in a local coffee shop to be a more palatable option than attending religious worship. Are such get-togethers the church?

Church is more than sharing fellowship among Christians, despite how meaningful those times can be. Church entails shared and outward signs, sacraments that guide and provide meaning and the presence of God among us.

30. See, e.g., Kevin J. Vanhoozer, *Biblical Authority after Babel: Retrieving the Solas in the Spirit of Mere Protestant Christianity* (Grand Rapids: Brazos, 2016).
31. "After 500 Years, Reformation-Era Divisions Have Lost Much of Their Potency," Pew Research Center, August 31, 2017, http://www.pewforum.org/2017/08/31/after-500-years-reformation-era-divisions-have-lost-much-of-their-potency.
32. "After 500 Years, Reformation-Era Divisions Have Lost Much of Their Potency."

In the words of Graham Ward, the church is known in its action, as a "body of action . . . for it is the body of Christ only in and through this continuous action."[33] As such, the church is, as Dulles puts it, "a fully visible society."[34] Such actions of this fully visible society are the stuff of sociological and anthropological research. Yet, invisibly and mysteriously, the church is active in that it shares in the life of the Triune God as the body of Christ active in the world today. There is a shared ontology—of Christ's presence—that binds members together. Furthermore, the church is an eschatological community, so that it is not satisfied just with the here and now but rather is geared toward the future (1 Pet. 5:10–11).

What, then, is the Christian church? "The Church is thus the means of Christ's work in the world; it is his hands and feet, his mouth and voice. As in his incarnate life, Christ had to have a body to proclaim his gospel and to do his work, so in his resurrection in this age he still needs a body to be the instrument of his gospel and of his work in the world."[35]

---

33. Graham Ward, *The Politics of Discipleship: Becoming Postmaterial Citizens* (Grand Rapids: Baker Academic, 2009), 201.

34. Dulles, *Models of the Church*, 9.

35. Alan Richardson, *An Introduction to the Theology of the New Testament* (New York: Harper, 1958), 256.

# 5

# How Do Christians Worship?

s a professor of world religions, I often tell my students that
one of the best ways to understand Christianity is to see Christians worship, rather than just relying on readings and discussions. There simply is no substitute. Why? Because worship expresses
worshipers' deepest convictions and beliefs about themselves, the
natural world, spiritual reality, and the Divine. Christian worship is
where Christians are encouraged and admonished, where they learn
about the Christian tradition, and from where they are sent out to
make a difference in our communities and the world.

Worship is the center of Christian life together. It is, in the words of
John Witvliet, "the locus of what several Christian traditions identify
as the nourishing center of congregational life: preaching, common
prayer, and the celebration of ordinances or sacraments."[1] For many
Christians, worship is the most significant reason why they join the
church, or why they leave it. Christian worship is a deal maker or
breaker. In Christian worship, we acknowledge God's greatness. We
honor God by praising and worshiping him because God alone de-
serves to be praised.

1. John Witvliet, series preface in *One Bread, One Body: Exploring Cultural Diversity in Worship*, ed. C. Michael Hawn (Herndon, VA: Alban Institute, 2003), xx.

You can find Christian worship that is quiet and Christian worship that is raucous and exuberant, and everything in between. In some parts of Asia persecuted Christians worship in silence, while in other parts Christians amplify their services using the latest technology so that as many as possible can hear. In Africa some Christians begin worship by processing in the streets, extending public invitations to be healed and to experience the power of God, while other African services employ quiet chanting based on traditions hundreds of years old. In North America many Christians display consumerist inclinations as they choose the right church that fits their particular preferences and lifestyles.

Recently, I took college students to visit the West Angeles Church of God in Christ, part of the largest black Pentecostal-Holiness denomination in the United States. Prior to the start of worship, one student noticed a woman walking back and forth in front of the large sanctuary, making movements with her arms as though she were sweeping with a broom. We learned that she was sweeping away evil influences prior to worship. You would not see this sort of cleansing in mainline Protestant churches in the West, where there is less emphasis on spiritual warfare. This example reflects the fact that Christian worship always entails cultural and spiritual elements. As such, Christian worship will look distinct in different cultural and socioeconomic environments. It is impossible to disconnect the two, flesh and spirit.

There are many forms of Christian worship. The procession in a Samoan traditional Catholic worship service might include the carrying of a fully cooked pig down the center aisle of the sanctuary. Eastern Orthodox worship involves lengthy periods of standing, sitting, and kneeling. A Pentecostal church in Seoul, South Korea, typically worships seven hours each Sunday but will worship nonstop for twenty-four hours every four weeks, with amplified instruments and charismatic preaching interspersed between energetic contemporary Christian music and intensely emotional times of confession and repentance. The celebrants in the Catholic Church in Mali process using the same dance forms they did in their pre-Christian religious practices, vigorously stamping their feet on the ground in a highly stylized fashion. The Cathedral of Christ the Light in Oakland, California, a beautiful yet simple Catholic cathedral, offers Mass in three languages, English, Spanish, and Vietnamese. Indeed, Christian worship is diverse.

It would be impossible to conceive of Christianity without Christian worship. The act of worship is essential to being Christian. Worship is a central part of all Christian churches. Because worship is crucial to being Christian, I start this chapter by suggesting that human beings are made to worship; what we worship gives us meaning and purpose. So I begin by defining what is unique about Christian worship. Second, I discuss various elements of Christian worship that are universal for most Christians across time and space. These include meeting weekly, public reading of the Bible, celebrating the Lord's Supper (e.g., Mass, Eucharist, Communion), the inclusion of music or song, prayer, teaching and preaching, and the sharing of offerings. Each church employs these features with greater or lesser intensity, with some, for instance, making the Lord's Supper the central act of worship (e.g., Catholic Church), while for others, song is central. The chapter closes with reflection on the helpful Nairobi Statement, which provides us with four features of healthy Christian worship, a practical lens through which to better understand Christian worship as either Christians or observers.

## What Is Worship?

Christianity teaches that all people worship. We are surrounded by distractions that vie for our attention and promise fulfillment. Whether those distractions are ideas, careers, relationships, or products, we are prone to make idols of them. Our proclivity is to give power to things and ideas that fundamentally do not possess the power to be of ultimate significance. In the Bible God states, "You shall have no other gods before me" (Exod. 20:3). These words challenge our general orientation to life so that we will not be attached to false gods, distractions, or any other idol. Yet, we are prone to worship false gods. This is why the Westminster Catechism of 1647 offers the biblical corrective: "[Our] chief end is to glorify God, and to enjoy Him forever."[2]

2. Westminster Shorter Catechism (1674), Christian Classics Ethereal Library, https://www.ccel.org/creeds/westminster-shorter-cat.html.

The Reformer Martin Luther exclaimed, "Whatever your heart clings to and confides in, that is really your god."[3] We are to worship God alone as God. Luther explained,

> A god is that to which we look for all good and where we resort for help in every time of need; to have a god is simply to trust and believe in one with our whole heart. As I have often said, the confidence and faith of the heart alone make both God and an idol. If your faith and confidence are right, then likewise your God is the true God. On the other hand, if your confidence is false, if it is wrong, then you have not the true God.[4]

Christianity would ask, Why would we seek for fulfillment apart from the Triune God, for in God we find whatever we lack?

Highlighting the universal need to worship, Tim Keller quotes the novelist David Foster Wallace, who told a graduating class at Kenyon College, "Everyone worships. The only choice we get is what to worship."[5] James K. A. Smith puts it this way: "We can't not worship because we can't not love *something* as ultimate."[6] Such is the condition that has marked our humanity (e.g., our minds and hearts) since the very beginning. In this context, then, it is stunning that God declares that he is the God who *first* loves us and delivered us to be in relationship to God, based not on our performance but by the grace of God through Jesus Christ. God, then, is not an object to be worshiped, but One with whom to be in relationship; worship is the response to that relationship. Rather than being initiated by us, Christian worship starts with the Triune God, who enlivens us so that we might worship him (Eph. 1:4–12).

If you were to ask your neighbor what Christian worship is, they might say something like, "singing in church," "listening to someone preach at me," or "learning morality." Christian worship is, indeed,

---

3. Martin Luther, *Luther's Large Catechism: God's Call to Repentance, Faith and Prayer*, trans. John Nicholas Lenker (Minneapolis: Luther Press, 1908), 44.

4. Luther, *Luther's Large Catechism*, 44.

5. Tim Keller, *Center Church: Doing Balanced, Gospel-Centered Ministry in Your City* (Grand Rapids: Zondervan, 2012), 34.

6. James K. A. Smith, *You Are What You Love: The Spiritual Power of Habit* (Grand Rapids: Brazos, 2016), 23.

"religious" since worship involves repetitive actions (e.g., liturgies) that are performed toward a given end—to honor God, to be spiritually nourished, and then to be sent out to share the gospel. Sometimes the patterns of worship can be quite formal, such as in Catholic or Eastern Orthodox worship, adorned with incense, candles, and ornate vestments. Or the patterns can be informal, such as in independent or pentecostal churches.[7] The origins of these rituals are fascinating, for they reflect a blending of biblical patterns, local culture, and nonlocal cultures. For instance, Christians in the New Guinea Highlands give offerings of the first fruits of their small gardens, usually consisting of sweet potatoes and various greens, for the pastor's consumption, while in many urban and suburban areas throughout the world it is increasingly popular to autodebit one's bank account to provide weekly offerings. I attended a church in China that received financial offerings via a huge QR code projected on the screen before worshipers. Despite the difference in style, all congregations make offerings of some sort.[8]

Christian worship means more than giving honor and respect to God. To paraphrase Mircea Eliade, worship opens communication between God and human beings and makes possible ontological passage from one mode of being to another.[9] Our very selves are involved when we worship. Worship ultimately entails divine participation. Worship provides that break in the normal activities of daily actions so that communication with God is established, for it is God who renders our deepest orientation possible.[10] Worship reorients us to what matters most, to what gives life, sustains, and guides us.

Worship was the background for so many of the events in the Bible. One of the most paradigmatic moments in the story of redemption,

7. I use "pentecostal" (lowercase "p") as an adjective to denote a style of worship that emphasizes the manifestation of the gifts of the Spirit, such as speaking in tongues, rather than "Pentecostal," which I use to refer to denominations with such emphases, such as the Assemblies of God, International Church of the Foursquare Gospel, or Church of God in Christ.

8. To learn about worship in various cultures around the world, see, e.g., Charles E. Farhadian, ed., *Christian Worship: Expanding Horizons, Deepening Practices* (Grand Rapids: Eerdmans, 2007); Hawn, *One Bread, One Body*.

9. Mircea Eliade, *The Sacred and the Profane: The Nature of Religion*, trans. Willard R. Trask (New York: Harcourt, Brace, 1959), 63.

10. Eliade, *The Sacred and the Profane*, 63.

and one that is reflected on so much today, was the exodus, when the Hebrew slaves fled Egypt. Recall that when the Lord called on Pharaoh to let God's people go, it was so that they might "worship" God (Exod. 9:13). Having been safely delivered through the Red Sea, Israel worshiped the Lord on Mount Sinai. Worship was so central to the well-being of the people that the book of Deuteronomy records the attempts to reform and purify Israel's worship. Prophets too kept reminding people to worship God alone.

Under the revelation of Jesus Christ, however, worship would no longer take place in the temple but rather in the body of Christ—the church—because Christians have become the temples of the Holy Spirit (1 Cor. 3:16–17; 6:19–20), with Christ as head (Eph. 1:22; Col. 1:18). While the earliest Christians, consisting mostly of Jews who recognized Jesus as the Messiah, continued to worship in the temple (Luke 24:53; Acts 2:46), distinctly Christian worship emerged as Christians met "in the name of Jesus," gathering together as a church. The most important practice they shared was the Lord's Supper (1 Cor. 11:17–34), both a recollection of the Jewish Passover and a remembrance and celebration of the new covenant brought by Jesus's death and resurrection. The Bible makes known that we are called to worship:

> Worship the LORD in the splendor of his holiness;
> tremble before him, all the earth. (Ps. 96:9)

Worship is shaped by liturgy—"the order of service." The term "liturgy" comes from the Greek word *leitourgia*, which means "the work of the people"; the actions of worship that we offer God constitute our liturgy.[11] Liturgy, then, involves rituals and actions, public celebrations, which are fundamentally a community's response to and participation in the saving work and life of the Triune God.

It is important to keep in mind that while liturgy is worship, not all worship is liturgy. Worship can be a private act, whereas liturgy is always a communal activity. Many Christians find it meaningful to

---

11. Constance Cherry, *The Worship Architect: A Blueprint for Designing Culturally Relevant and Biblically Faithful Services* (Grand Rapids: Baker Academic, 2010), 39.

worship daily or several times a week alone or with a small group of fellow believers; they worship by acknowledging and praising God. That is worship. Liturgy, on the other hand, involves a public gathering of people that includes rituals (e.g., sacraments), prayers, and praise.

All churches have liturgy, whether or not they use that term to describe their actions of worship. The main purpose of liturgy is to worship. In other words, both Pentecostal and Catholic churches have liturgy. When you visit a church, what is the order of the service and what actions do Christians take in the service? That is liturgy.

## What Is Involved in Christian Worship?

I enjoy visiting Christian worship services—of all kinds. To visit a small storefront evangelical church in Quito, Ecuador, an Aguaruna church in the Peruvian Amazon, an English-speaking congregation in Seoul, Korea, the spectacularly beautiful Westminster Cathedral in London or St. Peter's Basilica in Vatican City, a large pentecostal church in Los Angeles, or a church for prisoners in the state of Washington gives me a sense of awe at the immense diversity yet similarity of Christian worship around the world.

When I visit Christian worship services, the concept I take with me to help unpack what is going on is "carrier."[12] I borrow this term from sociologist Peter Berger, who uses it to explain what affects and alters the way people think. I apply the term "carrier" to worship to underscore the fact that every worship service contains elements that convey worship. "What carries this service?" The words? The song? The actions? The silence? The mystery? Sacraments, icons, music, choirs, robes, candles? What are the objects, words, architectures that carry Christian worship? And how do they function together to make worship meaningful?

Christian worship shares common features throughout the world. Christian worship in almost all churches entails at least (1) meeting weekly as an assembly; (2) reading portions of the Bible together;

12. Peter Berger, *The Homeless Mind* (New York: Vintage, 1973), 16.

(3) celebrating the Lord's Supper, whether weekly, monthly, quarterly, or some other regular pattern; (4) music or song; (5) prayer; (6) teaching and preaching; and (7) offering. These practices are done with various intensities and emphases, yet they all give shape to the practice of Christian worship. Before we consider these individual features of Christian worship, I want to make a few comments on what made Christian worship unique in the context of early Christianity in the Roman Empire.

Christian worship, while sharing some features of other religions in its place of origin in the Roman Empire, was distinctly different from Greco-Roman worship. Whereas Greco-Roman religious practices emphasized worship primarily of gods of the state, who offered "salvation" for the city rather than individuals and who cared little about human morality, early Christian worship focused on love of God and neighbor, stressing both corporate and individual morality.

Rodney Stark notes, "The chief emotional ingredient lacking in the traditional Roman faiths was *love*. Romans thought the gods might come to their aid, but they did not believe that the gods loved them—indeed Jupiter was depicted as quite unfriendly to human concerns."[13] Furthermore, Greco-Roman worship was a civic duty, whereas Christian worship was voluntary and, since it was perceived as a threat to the state and the powers that be, could very well lead to unrelenting persecution or death for worshipers.

### Meeting Weekly

The common features of Christian worship entail seven elements. First, Christian worship involves meeting weekly as an assembly.[14] There are good reasons why Christians would worship on Sunday. Sunday worship is rooted in creation itself, where God, after creating, established a day of rest, calling that day holy (Gen. 2:3): "It will be a sign between me and the Israelites forever, for in six days the LORD made the heavens and the earth, and on the seventh day

---

13. Rodney Stark, *The Triumph of Christianity: How the Jesus Movement Became the World's Largest Religion* (San Francisco: HarperOne, 2011), 18.

14. This practice stands in stark contrast with the early church, consisting of Jews in Jerusalem, who met every day in the temple and in private homes (Acts 2:46; 5:42).

he rested and was refreshed" (Exod. 31:17). "Refresh" conveys the image of a king who has completed his work and, after taking his throne, finds joy and satisfaction in his creation (Ps. 104:31). In the Bible, the Sabbath, a day set aside for rest and worship, was the day when people celebrated God's forgiveness and redemption (Lev. 16:30–31; Deut. 5:12–15). Jews kept the Sabbath from Friday evening to Saturday evening, but the majority of Christians observe the Sabbath on Sunday.

Furthermore, Jesus Christ rose from the dead on the first day of the week—Sunday—overcoming sin by dying for all (Rom. 5:12–19). When Paul desired to collect an offering from the church at Corinth, he requested that they gather the money on the "first day of the week" (1 Cor. 16:2). In Troas, Paul greeted gathered believers on the first day of the week when they broke (ate) bread together (Acts 20:7). In the first century, Ignatius described Christians with a Jewish background as those who "have come to the possession of a new hope, no longer observing the Sabbath [Saturday], but living in the observance of the Lord's Day, on which also our life has sprung up again by Him and by His death."[15] In the second century, Justin Martyr wrote one of the earliest descriptions of specifically Christian worship in his *First Apology*:

> And on the day called Sunday, all who live in cities or in the country gather together to one place, and the memoirs of the apostles or the writings of the prophets are read, as long as time permits; then, when the reader has ceased, the president verbally instructs, and exhorts to the imitation of these good things. Then we all rise together and pray, and, as we before said, when our prayer is ended, bread and wine and water are brought, and the president in like manner offers prayers and thanksgivings, according to his ability, and the people assent, saying Amen. . . . For [Christ] was crucified on the day before that of Saturn (Saturday); and on the day after that of Saturn, which is the day of the Sun, having appeared to His apostles and disciples, He taught them these things, which we have submitted to you also for your consideration.[16]

15. Ignatius, *To the Magnesians* 9.1, http://www.newadvent.org/fathers/0105.htm.
16. Justin Martyr, *First Apology* 67, http://www.newadvent.org/fathers/0126.htm.

Although the vast majority of Christians worship on Sundays, some worship on Saturday (e.g., Seventh-day Adventists), based mainly on their adherence to the fourth commandment to work the first six days of the week and to rest on the seventh (Exod. 20:8–11).

### Public Bible Reading

A second common feature of Christian worship is the reading of portions of the Bible together. Reading Scripture has been practiced since before the beginning of the church, when Jewish believers in the Messiah would gather together to read as a part of public worship in the synagogue. The Old Testament is replete with examples of Jews reading Scripture as a way to remind them of God's character, presence, and promises. For instance, when Solomon's temple was being rebuilt (458 BCE), "all the people came together as one in the square below the Water Gate. They told Ezra the teacher of the Law to bring the Book of the Law of Moses, which the LORD had commanded for Israel" (Neh. 8:1), and then they "read from the Book of the Law of God, making it clear and giving the meaning so that the people understood what was being read" (Neh. 8:8).

The New Testament recounts several occasions when the reading of Scriptures, particularly from the Law, the Psalms, and Prophets played a central role in worship. The Gospel of Luke recounts Jesus on the Sabbath entering the synagogue and, receiving the scroll of the prophet Isaiah, unrolling it and reading from it, proclaiming that Scripture was fulfilled in him (Luke 4:14–21). Paul told Timothy in Ephesus, "Until I come, devote yourself to the public reading of Scripture, to preaching and to teaching" (1 Tim. 4:13). The significance of the Bible and the public reading of it in Christian worship are illustrated by the fact that, as Eusebius (263–399 CE) notes, during the Diocletian persecution of Christians in the Roman Empire, Scriptures and liturgical books were burned.[17] Roman authorities recognized the source of Christian living.

What specific portions of the Bible are read in Christian worship? Some Christian traditions read Scripture according to lectionaries,

17. Eusebius, *Ecclesiastical History* 8.2.4.

which are lists that give selections of the Bible that are appointed to be read on a given Sunday. Roman Catholic, Eastern Orthodox, Anglican, and several mainline Protestant churches use lectionaries to guide their weekly reading and preaching. *The Roman Catholic Mass Lectionary*, which is the basis for many mainline Protestant lectionaries, follows a pattern of four elements of public reading each Sunday: (1) reading from the Old Testament, (2) responsorial psalm, (3) reading from one of the New Testament Letters, and (4) Gospel reading.

Many churches do not follow a lectionary and instead publicly read the portion of Scripture that corresponds to the preaching for that week. You can imagine the positive and negative aspects of either approach. Using a lectionary gives a worshiper a sense of continuity and connection among congregations as he or she travels or moves to different locations. Those who do not use lectionaries have the flexibility to read selections of Scripture that might be more pertinent to a given crisis, need, or celebration in the church and wider community.

Through the public reading of Scripture we have the opportunity to hear from God in a personal way that touches our hearts, minds, emotions, and spirits. The Bible says that God's Word convicts, encourages, comforts, and guides.[18] As we are quiet and hear the reading, we have space to reflect and listen to God speak to us directly through the Holy Spirit.

### Celebrating the Lord's Supper

One of the most meaningful yet historically divisive aspects of Christian worship is the celebration of the Lord's Supper, called Communion, Eucharist, or Mass depending on the Christian tradition. The typical elements used in Communion are bread, representing Christ's body, and wine (or grape juice), representing his blood. The origin of the sacrament of the Lord's Supper was when Jesus shared his final meal with his disciples in an upper room in Jerusalem on the night before his crucifixion. This was the occasion of the institution

---

18. See, e.g., Josh. 1:9; Prov. 3:5–6; 18:10; Isa. 40:31; 43:2; John 14:27; 2 Cor. 1:3–4; 1 Thess. 4:18; 2 Tim. 3:16; Heb. 4:12; 1 Pet. 5:7.

of the Lord's Supper. The bread and wine are consecrated, set aside for God's purpose, on an altar or table, and then consumed by Christians during worship. The biblical Greek term *eucharistia* ("Eucharist") means simply "thanksgiving." It does not refer to a ritual but is found in the New Testament description of the practice of sharing bread and wine together in remembrance of Jesus Christ.

The term "Eucharist" was used in the early church and is employed today by Roman Catholics, Eastern Orthodox, Anglicans, Presbyterians, and Lutherans. The use of the term "Lord's Supper" first occurred in the mid-first century, with the words, "So then, when you come together, it is not the Lord's Supper you eat, for when you are eating, some of you go ahead with your own private suppers" (1 Cor. 11:20–21a). The term "Mass" is used by the Roman Catholic Church and some Lutheran and Anglican churches to refer to the longer ritual that consists of the Liturgy of the Word, Liturgy of the Eucharist, and Concluding Rite. Therefore, Mass consists of Bible readings, a brief sermon, celebration of the Eucharist, and final prayers and blessings.

A major issue that has led to division within the church concerns the elements of the Lord's Supper—that is, the bread and the wine. What do Jesus's words "This is my body" (Matt. 26:26) mean? How churches have answered this question has given rise to tensions within the church since the time of the Reformation. The question concerning the Lord's Supper was centered on the "real presence" of Jesus in the elements (bread and wine). What does "real presence" mean? What about Jesus's phrases "This is my body" and "This is my blood"?[19]

In a mid-fourth-century statement, Cyril of Jerusalem lectured that the bread and wine somehow became the body and blood of Christ, and believers, by partaking in those elements, partake in the divine nature itself.

> Wherefore with full assurance let us partake as of the Body and Blood of Christ: for in the figure of Bread is given to you His Body, and in the figure of Wine His Blood; that you by partaking of the Body and Blood of Christ, may be made of the same body and the same blood

19. See Matt. 26:26–28; Mark 14:22–24; Luke 22:19–20; 1 Cor. 11:23–26.

with Him. For thus we come to bear Christ in us, because His Body and Blood are distributed through our members; thus it is that, according to the blessed Peter, we become partakers of the divine nature.[20]

Church leaders in the Middle Ages held a variety of views regarding the Lord's Supper. In the early eighth century, John of Damascus affirmed that the mystery of the bread and wine changed to the body and blood of Christ, being content that the Holy Spirit comes upon the elements and achieves what surpasses our human knowledge. John of Damascus was less concerned about the details of this change. A debate in the ninth century in a monastery in Corbie, France, between monks Radbertus and Ratramnus, illustrated the church's thinking about the "real presence." Radbertus argued that the ordinary bread and wine transformed into the body and blood of Christ, whereas Ratramnus argued that the "difference between ordinary and consecrated bread lay in the way in which the believer perceived them."[21] Was change in the elements or in the heart of the believer?

During the Reformation, the debate about the "real presence" led to the different interpretations known today as transubstantiation, consubstantiation, and memorialism, perspectives that distinguish today's church denominations. Transubstantiation means that the substance of bread and wine actually changes into the body and blood of Jesus Christ, even while their physical traits remain. Here the real substantial presence of Christ is affirmed, where the whole substance of the bread and wine transforms into the body and blood of Christ. Roman Catholics hold this view.

A second approach is that of consubstantiation, whereby the bread and wine are both bread and wine as well as the body and blood of Christ at one and the same time. While there is no change in substance, Christ is fully present in the elements. Martin Luther famously provided an analogy for this view by describing an iron put into the fire whereby both fire and iron are united in the red-hot iron and yet each continues unchanged.[22] Lutherans and Anglicans identify with this position.

A third major viewpoint, usually referred to as memorialism and associated with Swiss Reformed leader Huldrych Zwingli, understood the Lord's Supper to be a memorial of the suffering of Jesus Christ. Thus, "This is my body" should be taken metaphorically or figuratively. In this view, then, taking the bread and wine is a commemoration of the sacrificial death of Christ, but Christ himself is not directly present in the sacrament. Many Protestant denominations, such as free-church Protestants and Baptist churches, hold this perspective.

### Music or Song

Singing has always been a vital part of Christian worship. It is surprising to realize that song existed at the moment of creation itself:

> On what were its footings set,
>    or who laid its cornerstone—
> while the morning stars sang together
>    and all the angels shouted for joy? (Job 38:6–7)

After escaping from the Egyptians and crossing the Red Sea, the Hebrews sang a song to the Lord (Exod. 15:1–21). The book of Psalms is a compilation of songs and hymns for God's work in creation and history, to express communal and individual laments, thanksgivings, and praise of God. Song frames the beginning and the consummation of time (Rev. 5:11–14).

Song is so integral to Christian worship that it distinguished Christians from their early contemporaries since Christian worship was filled with liveliness, robust sound, and body movement. Rodney Stark notes the difference between early Christian worship and other kinds of worship prevalent in the first century: "In contrast, the new faith stressed celebration, joy, ecstasy, and passion. Music played a leading role in their services—not only flutes and horns, but an abundance of group singing and dancing. As for ecstasy, the behavior

---

22. F. L. Cross, ed., *The Oxford Dictionary of the Christian Church* (London: Oxford University Press, 2005), 411.

of participants in the worship of some of these groups sounds very like modern Pentecostalism—people going into trancelike states and speaking in unknown tongues."[23]

In the New Testament, a significant feature of the Christian response to Jesus Christ is song. For instance, there are three canticles (hymns or songs of praise) that appear in the opening chapters of the Gospel of Luke. These praise hymns are still used in churches today. First, the Magnificat, also known as the Song of Mary (Luke 1:46–55), is Mary's responsive song to the announcement shared with her by the angel Gabriel that she would give birth to the Christ. Her song begins,

> My soul glorifies the Lord
>    and my spirit rejoices in God my Savior,
> for he has been mindful
>    of the humble state of his servant.
> From now on all generations will call me blessed,
>    for the Mighty One has done great things for me—
>    holy is his name. (Luke 1:46–49)

A second song of praise, the Benedictus, also known as the Song of Zechariah (Luke 1:68–79), likewise occurs in the early part of the Gospel of Luke within the context of the annunciation. The Benedictus is the song of thanksgiving uttered by Zechariah when his son, who would become known as John the Baptizer, was circumcised. The Benedictus begins,

> Praise be to the Lord, the God of Israel,
>    because he has come to his people and redeemed them.
> He has raised up a horn of salvation for us
>    in the house of his servant David. (Luke 1:68–69)

This is a song of thanksgiving for the messianic hopes of the Jewish people. A third canticle in the Gospel of Luke is the Nunc Dimittis, also known as the Song of Simeon (Luke 2:29–32). This song is offered by Simeon, who had been promised by the Holy Spirit that he

23. Stark, *Triumph of Christianity*, 18.

would not die until he had seen the Messiah. Upon seeing the infant Jesus in the temple in Jerusalem, Simeon took the baby in his arms and exclaimed:

> Sovereign Lord, as you have promised,
>     you may now dismiss your servant in peace.
> For my eyes have seen your salvation,
>     which you have prepared in the sight of all nations:
> a light for revelation to the Gentiles,
>     and the glory of your people Israel. (Luke 2:29–32)

Sung in Roman Catholic, Orthodox, and Anglican churches, the Magnificat and the Benedictus are the traditional canticles of Morning Prayer (Matins), focused on praise, and Evening Prayer (Evensong), focused on thanksgiving. The Nunc Dimittis is sung in evening worship, such as Compline, Vespers, and Evensong. Compline, or Night Prayer, is sung before going to bed, around 9:00 p.m. Vespers, or Evening Prayer, is sung around 6:00 p.m. It is worthwhile to note that song in early Christian worship consisted mostly of melody only, without accompanying harmony or chords.

Toward the end of the Middle Ages, more complex musical styles, with more melody lines, were composed for use in worship. In the ninth and tenth centuries, Gregorian chants were created as part of the Christian liturgies of the Roman Catholic Church. Orthodox churches likewise use a variety of ancient worship chants.

During the Reformation, Protestant church music varied considerably, from the rejection of instruments and acceptance of only singing to the extensive use of instruments and large choirs. This variety was based mostly on theological differences. Early Lutherans, for instance, believed that God's grace could be experienced through instruments and songs, not from song in the Bible alone, whereas early Calvinists believed that the use of instruments and songs, other than from the Psalter (Psalms), distracted Christians.

Many of the well-known Reformation and post-Reformation leaders, such as John and Charles Wesley, Martin Luther, and Isaac Watts, also composed hymns that were adopted by the church. John Calvin advocated singing only from the book of Psalms, as well as the Lord's Prayer and the Apostles' Creed, because he believed that Christians should sing only the words that God had given them through Scripture:

> Now what Saint Augustine says is true, that no one is able to sing things worthy of God unless he has received them from Him.
>
> Wherefore, when we have looked thoroughly everywhere and searched high and low, we shall find no better songs nor more appropriate to the purpose than the psalms of David which the Holy Spirit made and spoke through him. And furthermore, when we sing them, we are certain that God puts the words in our mouths, as if He Himself were singing in us to exalt His glory.[24]

The late twentieth and early twenty-first centuries have witnessed a massive rise in the styles of music and the ways in which those forms are disseminated worldwide. Musical content and styles are showing signs of becoming increasingly homogeneous, as globalization and commercialization enable worship songs to merge with forces of the market and channels of promotion and distribution via the Internet to be adopted around the world.

For instance, contemporary Christian music (CCM) has generated a large, independent, and financially successful industry, complete with published and recorded music, copyright licensing procedures, magazines, and conferences. CCM is supported by a vast network of Christian radio and Internet stations and has generated a roster of celebrity musicians and composers. CCM is in part a market-driven industry that keeps its ear close to the ground to learn what sells and adjusts to that market. Some are critical of CCM, but for others it is the only worship music they have known, and it is meaningful and uplifting. One thing is for sure—CCM's global reach profoundly shapes Christian worship around the world.

There are important questions to ask ourselves as we try to understand Christian worship. What role do elements of local culture play in worship music? What are the most appropriate ways of adopting features of cultures from different worshiping communities?

---

24. John Calvin, *John Calvin: Writings on Pastoral Piety*, trans. Elsie Anne McKee (Mahwah, NJ: Paulist Press, 2001), 96.

On a visit to a Karen church near the Thailand-Burma border several years ago, I was surprised to see Karen believers, dressed in traditional Karen clothing, singing contemporary Christian music popular in the United States, using amplified instruments and microphones. This scene is increasingly familiar, as churches in Asia, Africa, Latin America, and the Pacific are adopting musical styles and instrumentation from the Global North. What we do not see are local cultural forms, such as Thai bamboo flutes and Chinese single-stringed instruments, being played in churches in the United States. The global flow of music, song, and instrumentation is changing the face of the church worldwide. And that flow is strongly unidirectional, traveling from the Global North to the Global South.

Despite the complications caused by globalization, congregational song remains essential to Christian worship. Constance Cherry, summarizing the insights of Brian Wren and Ralph P. Martin, suggests six reasons for the indispensability of song in worship: we sing because the church was born in song; we sing because there is a biblical mandate for corporate singing in worship; we sing because it is a primary communal activity; we sing because it is inclusive; we sing because it is a vehicle for expressing our faith; and we sing because it provides much inspiration for the community.[25]

### Prayer

Some Christians approach God like God is some kind of candy man. Christians ask; God gives. All Christians pray, yet what is prayer? Is it asking God for things we want? Christians are enjoined to pray individually (Matt. 6:6) and corporately (Acts 1:14). In fact, in the New Testament prayer is commanded (Col. 4:2; 1 Thess. 5:17) because prayer enables intimacy with God, reminds us of our place in creation, and is essential for our well-being. Prayer involves our entire being—heart, mind, and spirit—with the goal of seeking union with God. The Bible describes the function of prayer as a way to call to

---

25. Cherry, *The Worship Architect*, 155–56. An excellent introduction to singing in the worshiping church is C. Michael Hawn, *Gather into One: Praying and Singing Globally* (Grand Rapids: Eerdmans, 2003).

God (Matt. 6:9–13), to intercede (James 5:13–16), to consult (1 Sam. 28:6), and to cry out (Ps. 77:1).

Early church fathers, such as John of Damascus, wrote of prayer as elevating the mind to God. Gregory of Nyssa explained that prayer is communion and conversation with God. John Chrysostom saw prayer as talking with God. Prayer is action and the way by which we communicate with God since God promises to hear us and respond (1 John 5:14–15).

Since its birth, the church has prayed corporately. Immediately after Jesus was taken up into heaven, the disciples "all joined together constantly in prayer, along with the women and Mary the mother of Jesus, and with his brothers" (Acts 1:14). They all, women and men, prayed together. Corporate prayer is indispensable in worship because God desires for his people to be one (John 17:23). The centrality of prayer is so important that the entire worship service could be said to be a prayer to God.

In Christian worship there are typically three kinds of prayer: liturgical, extemporaneous, and charismatic-pentecostal. Liturgical prayer is public prayer that is prescribed, often with physical gestures (e.g., crossing oneself or kneeling) and use of objects (e.g., palms, candles). Liturgical prayers follow prescribed ritual formulas. These kinds of prayers are used in highly liturgical churches, such as Catholic, Eastern Orthodox, Lutheran, and Anglican.

Extemporaneous prayers, which are popular among evangelical churches, are unscripted. These prayers can be short or long. Because of their informality, extemporaneous prayers are said without referring to written or preformulated prayers. Charismatic-pentecostal prayers are extemporaneous, yet they emphasize the "leading by the Holy Spirit," based, for instance, on the biblical promise that the Holy Spirit intercedes for believers through speaking in tongues, an unknown language that the Spirit inspires for individual and corporate edification (Rom. 8:26–27). Glossolalia, or "speaking in tongues" (1 Cor. 12:10, 28), is a gift of the Holy Spirit and an important marker of pentecostal, Spirit-led prayer.

Charismatic-pentecostal prayer reminds us of one of the most important features of corporate prayer: it is a way to engage in spiritual warfare (Eph. 6:12). Christians recognize that corporate prayer contends against forces of evil in order to gain victory (2 Cor. 10:4; 1 Tim. 1:18). Therefore, in corporate worship prayer provides mutual encouragement, and it is where Christians contend against evil, grow in intimacy with God, are reassured of God's promises, and experience conviction by the Holy Spirit that leads to repentance.

### Teaching and Preaching

Historically, Christians received their knowledge of Christian tradition through the church, where they learned the catechism (the church's teaching) and its implications for Christian living. On a basic level, teaching and preaching in Christian worship are geared toward preparing people for active participation in the liturgy of the church—for example, by helping people understand the nature of the church, its beliefs, symbols, and practices. The focus of preaching in the context of Christian worship is the proclamation of the *kerygma*, a Greek word referring to the apostolic proclamation of salvation through Jesus Christ. Preaching the *kerygma* expresses the message of Jesus's entire ministry, with the aim of declaring Jesus Christ as Lord. Simply put, the *kerygma* is summarized as the good news of peace with God through Jesus the Messiah, who is Lord of all. While some churches would not directly preach the *kerygma*, the basic elements of it are celebrated in their liturgies in the overall drama of worship.

Beyond the proclamation of the gospel, Christian worship entails teaching about a host of biblical passages and theological topics. In liturgical churches that utilize a lectionary, sermons are based primarily on the Bible readings for that week, whereas in churches that do not use lectionaries, preaching can be on any variety of topics or biblical passages. Topics can include just about anything—politics, sex, family life, wisdom, widowhood, lust, history, economics, violence, Satan, spirituality, love, theology, idolatry, adventure, slavery, virtues, immorality, God, or gardening. These might sound like an odd lot, but they and other topics are in the Bible and eventually make their way into sermons.

Preaching styles differ. In churches whose worship is charismatic-pentecostal, the pastor might offer a sermon in a singsong rhythm with high performance aesthetic. Other churches are more rational in their approach and rhetorical appeal.

In charismatic and independent or evangelical churches, sermons can last forty-five to sixty minutes. In other church traditions, such as in more highly liturgical churches (e.g., Roman Catholic, Anglican, Orthodox), sermons can be brief, maybe ten to fifteen minutes. One reason for this is quite practical: the rich liturgical traditions of these churches take time. Roman Catholic and Orthodox churches, for instance, practice the oldest form of preaching, the homily. A homily is a short commentary on some part of Scripture, without introduction, to explain the spiritual meaning of that text. Nowadays Catholic priests are encouraged to limit their homilies to less than eight minutes, in order to keep the attention of the members of the congregation.

Congregational responses to sermons differ as well, with some being utterly quiet and others vocally engaged, shouting "Amen" or other words of encouragement and confirmation when the sermon hits home. In rural New Guinea, it is not surprising during the sermon for members of the congregation to interject questions that the pastor is expected to answer during the sermon. You can imagine how lively those churches can be.

### Offering

Jesus spoke more about money than he did about love. How we use or abuse or are abused by money conveys something about the state of our hearts. It is not surprising that the love of money seems a universal problem. It is not money itself that seems to be at issue, for Jesus taught the legitimate use of money. It is our orientation toward money that matters. God commanded his people to bring tithes and offerings (Mal. 3:6–12); Jesus taught that we ought to pay our taxes (Matt. 17:24–27) but to "give back to Caesar what is Caesar's, and to God what is God's" (Matt. 22:17–22). It is far too easy for people to depend on their own resources rather than trusting God to meet their needs (Matt. 6:9–13; Luke 12:22–34).

Based on Old Testament teaching, a tithe is the first 10 percent of one's income, which God calls a Christian to give to his or her local church each month.[26] Some people follow this practice literally, while others believe it to indicate giving a portion of his or her resources (not necessarily money) to one's local congregation. An offering, on the other hand, is any money that a Christian chooses to give above and beyond the tithe. Tithes and offerings help in practical ways the functioning of the church, its staff, and property. Tithes and offerings are also distributed, ideally, to those in need in the local community, nation, and world. Tithes and offerings also support the mission efforts of the church.

Giving tithes and offerings is an act of Christian worship, not a business transaction. We respond to God through our act of giving, demonstratively acknowledging that all we possess and are is from God. We give not because we owe God anything but because we recognize that we have been purchased with a price (1 Cor. 6:20) and all that we have is a gift from God. So we give back to God with an attitude of thanksgiving. By giving tithes and offerings in worship, Christians demonstrate that our identities are tied up not in our own accomplishments, statuses, and wealth but in the God who restores our world and ourselves. Finally, tithing in the Bible is connected to justice. Jesus criticized the Pharisees, who tithed faithfully yet neglected justice and the love of God (Luke 11:42), and called for both giving tithes and doing justice.

The church has been wracked with abuse when it comes to money. Such abuse has also been a part of the history of the church. The "prosperity gospel," the belief that financial and physical blessings are guaranteed for those who give money to the church, is present on every continent. Church leaders promoting the prosperity gospel exclaim that it is God's will for people to be materially wealthy and happy, which includes the alleviation of illness and material poverty. These so-called curses can be broken by making a donation to the church, they say. As such, you can imagine that churches promoting a "prosperity gospel" strongly emphasize the importance of financial giving. Historian Carter Lindberg parallels the prosperity gospel with the

26. Many Christians base their logic of tithing 10 percent on Gen. 14:20, when Abraham gave a tenth of his spoils of war to Melchizedek, or Deut. 14:22–26, when a tenth of Israel's fruit, seed, and flocks were given to the Lord.

medieval indulgence trade, whereby greedy church commissaries would extract the maximum amount of money for each indulgence that they promised would remit the giver's sin and punishment before God.[27]

Despite the potential for abuse, giving tithes and offerings can be one of the most meaningful parts of Christian worship, as we acknowledge our dependence on and gratefulness to God for our lives and sustenance. We also get to see how God uses those gifts to benefit others.

## Nairobi Statement

I conclude this chapter with a helpful statement on Christian worship, one that we can employ as observers, visitors, liturgists, worship planners, or members of the church. The Nairobi Statement comes from the meeting of the Lutheran World Federation's Study Team on Worship and Culture, held in Nairobi, Kenya, in January of 1996.[28] Beginning with the acknowledgment that Christian worship is the heart and pulse of the church, the Nairobi Statement presents four ways in which worship relates dynamically to culture.

First, Christian worship is *transcultural*. That is, the resurrected Christ, by whom we know the Triune God, transcends all cultures: there is one Bible, translated into many languages; one Lord's Supper; and one grand narrative of Christ's birth, death, resurrection, sending of the Spirit, and our baptism into him.

Second, Christian worship is *contextual*. Jesus was born into a specific culture of the world, thus exemplifying the contextualization of Christian worship. A culture's values and patterns, as long as they are consonant with the gospel, ought to be used to express the meaning and purpose of Christian worship.

27. Carter Lindberg, *The European Reformations* (Malden, MA: Wiley-Blackwell, 2010), 59–60.

28. Rather than providing several footnotes in this section, I ask readers to note that my reflections here are based on the Nairobi Statement on Worship and Culture, which can be found in Charles E. Farhadian, ed., *Christian Worship Worldwide: Expanding Horizons, Deepening Practices* (Grand Rapids: Eerdmans, 2007), 285–90; or see https://worship.calvin.edu/resources/resource-library/nairobi-statement-on -worship-and-culture-full-text.

Third, Christian worship is *countercultural*. Jesus Christ came to transform all people and all cultures. Nothing stays the same under the revelation of Christ. Some components of every culture are sinful, dehumanizing, and contradictory to the gospel. Therefore, the gospel both judges and endorses elements of culture, ultimately transforming cultural patterns, the idolization of self, and false hopes in order to empower the church to actively engage the world with the gospel of Christ.

Finally, Christian worship is *cross-cultural*. Jesus came to be the Lord and Savior of all people. Jesus welcomes the treasures, insights, beauty, and wisdom of cultures into worship.[29] The sharing of hymns, art, prayers, biblical insights, and other elements of worship across cultures helps enrich the whole church and strengthen the communion of the church worldwide. In doing so, we ought to be careful that the music, art, gestures, insights, and other elements of different cultures are understood and respected when used in churches elsewhere.

Until this point we have considered Christianity's past and present. What about the future of Christianity? Where are its growing edges? In the next chapter I offer comments on the possible futures of Christianity.

---

29. See, e.g., Andrew Walls, "The Ephesians Moment in Worldwide Worship: A Meditation on Revelation 21 and Ephesians 2," in Farhadian, *Christian Worship Worldwide*, 27–37.

# 6

# Where Is Christianity Going?

In 1907, in what today is the capital of North Korea, Pyongyang, the Great Revival of 1907 erupted, giving rise to a dramatic increase in the numbers of Christians and a transformation of nearly every aspect of Korean society. Just two years prior, in 1905, the Pyongyang mission consisted of an array of religious, educational, and medical institutions, such as the Union Children's Hospital, Union Christian College, and Union Presbyterian Theological Seminary. Around that time, the roughly two hundred American missionaries included professors, medical doctors, clergy, and administrators at the medical school, seminary, and college.

The history of the Great Revival of 1907 started in January of that year with a missionary-led, two-week Bible study in Pyongyang. Following each evening's class, missionaries extended an invitation for people to come forward and confess their sins. They did so but in a lackluster and apparently insincere manner. However, on the second-to-last night of the study, a revival occurred. What happened was that one after another, men went forward to the front and confessed their personal sins, weeping and wailing as they did so, their voices praying in unison into the night. The following night, the emotionally charged confessions continued with greater intensity.

By 1911, the number of ordained Korean pastors surpassed the number of ordained missionaries. Among those Koreans ordained in 1907 was Kil Sun-joo (Gil Seon-ju), a key figure in the Pyongyang Revival, who introduced the spiritual practice of early morning prayers. Kil Sun-joo, one of the first Presbyterian ministers in Korea, is considered by many to be the father of Korean Christianity. He later became a major figure in Korean nationalism, the March 1st Independence Movement, and a signer of the Korean declaration of independence.

The Pyongyang Revival lasted forty years and influenced almost every element of Korean life; it led to the city being called the "Jerusalem of the East" among missionaries. The Pyongyang Revival introduced key aspects of Korean Christian spirituality, such as early morning prayer and all-night prayer. Every single important Korean communist in the 1920s to the 1940s came from a Christian family influenced by the Pyongyang Revival. Following the Great Revival, illiterate people began to learn to read the Bible and missionary schools and hospitals were built.

However, with the division of the Korean Peninsula into two states in 1945, most Korean Christians in the north fled to the south to escape persecution from the new communist regime. Nearly seventy-five years later, there are few Christian churches in North Korea, and reports say that North Korea has the most ruthless persecution of Christians in the world, with Christians there being routinely imprisoned, raped, starved, and executed.

Just one year before the Pyongyang Revival of 1907, a similar revival erupted in Los Angeles, California. Known as the Azusa Street Revival, the movement was led by black American pastor William Joseph Seymour. In 1906, Seymour and his group found an abandoned African Methodist Church on Azusa Street, where he held worship services three times a day, seven days a week, from 1906 to 1909, in the dilapidated mission they called Apostolic Faith. The message of Seymour and his followers was straightforward: you can receive baptism of the Holy Spirit just as the apostles did on the day of Pentecost. Speaking in tongues was evidence of this pentecostal infilling. The Azusa Street Revival would become a major turning point in Christianity worldwide.

The Azusa Street Revival birthed modern Pentecostal movements and denominations. It is important to note that Spirit-led pentecostal experiences were happening prior to 1906 in other countries (e.g., Wales, India, Chile, Australia), yet some of the largest Pentecostal denominations today are connected historically to the Azusa Street Revival. These Pentecostals believed in a third blessing for Christians, the pentecostal experience, to go along with salvation and the Wesleyan teaching of entire sanctification (a moment of giving oneself over entirely to the Triune God). Some of the denominations that emerged either directly or indirectly from the Azusa Street Revival include the Assemblies of God (Missouri), the Pentecostal Church of God (Missouri), and the International Church of the Foursquare Gospel (California).

Of course, the pentecostal experience is not a modern phenomenon. The first Christians spoke in tongues through the baptism of the Holy Spirit (Acts 2:1–12). The Holy Spirit worked powerfully throughout the history of the church, demonstrating God's presence through miracles and other signs.[1] Around the time of the Azusa Street Revival, other healing revivals occurred—for instance, on the Ivory Coast and in Ghana (1914–15), Nigeria (1930), and China (1930–32). Commenting on the global impact of the Azusa Street Revival, Pentecostal scholar Allan Anderson notes, "Pentecostal missionaries were sent from Azusa Street to China, India, Japan, Egypt, Liberia, Angola, and South Africa. . . . The first missionaries from Azusa Street were convinced that they had been given missionary tongues through the baptism in the Spirit. They believed that when they reached their destinations they would miraculously speak foreign tongues without needing to undergo the arduous task of language learning."[2]

Pentecostalism is among the fastest-growing religious movements in the world. Its explosive growth and influence have captured the attention of both the church and the academy. The University of Southern California (USC), for instance, oversaw a multimillion-dollar research program trying to understand how Pentecostals have exerted

1. See, e.g., Craig S. Keener, *Miracles: The Credibility of the New Testament Accounts*, 2 vols. (Grand Rapids: Baker Academic, 2011).

2. Allan Anderson, "To All Points of the Compass: The Azusa Street Revival and Global Pentecostalism," *Enrichment Journal* 11, no. 2 (2006): 167.

influence in economic, religious, and political spheres of society. The USC program employed researchers in more than twenty countries in an attempt to understand Pentecostalism's impact around the world. USC is not alone in doing research on the social, cultural, economic, political, and religious impact of Pentecostalism; research centers also exist in Latin America, Asia, and Africa.

Given the preceding examples of North Korea and California, we must consider important questions when we think about the future of Christianity. How might Christianity fare in the future in these locations, Pyongyang and Los Angeles? Will Christianity grow again in North Korea and decrease in the United States? What were the conditions that gave rise to the Pyongyang Revival? What is the relationship between Christianity and state power? How did Christianity inspire Koreans to be active in the independence movement and to be signers of the North Korean declaration of independence? How did personal confession impact the burgeoning of Christianity? The case of the Azusa Street Revival raises a host of different questions: What role does globalization, and in particular technology and later the Internet, play in advancing or diminishing the growth of Christianity? Relatedly, in what ways do laws and politics enable Christianity to flourish?

In the Pyongyang and Azusa Street Revivals at least two things are in play: the role of the Holy Spirit and structures that either impede or promote Christianity. The influence of the Holy Spirit cannot be overlooked. To be faithful to Christianity, we need to take seriously the actions of the Spirit of God in changing people and societies. Finally, when we consider the edges of Christian growth, it is wise to remember that other expressions of Christianity, along with Pentecostalism, are thriving.

## Speaking about Numbers

As I mentioned in an earlier chapter, I find it unhelpful to rely too heavily on numbers alone when trying to understand the state and influence of Christianity—or any religion, for that matter. Nevertheless, numbers do tell us something important about the condition of Christianity today and in the near future. As we review these projections, we ought to see them as hints of possible changes afoot. Why only hints? For many obvious reasons, not the least of which is that human beings do not know where the Spirit of God will move and how the political and cultural climate may change in various regions. As the Bible explains, "The wind blows wherever it pleases. You hear its sound, but you cannot tell where it comes from or where it is going. So it is with everyone born of the Spirit" (John 3:8). Needless to say, there are countless stories in history where the best efforts of Christians to enliven and grow the church have failed. And there are countless examples of the opposite, where small gatherings of believers developed rapidly into massive churches or Christian movements, or where once stagnant churches were invigorated and became major sources of social and spiritual uplift in their communities.

Since the early twentieth century, Christianity has become geographically more diverse, being less concentrated in Europe and more evenly distributed throughout the Americas, the Asia-Pacific region, and sub-Saharan Africa. Why the change? Can we blame skeptical approaches to the Bible, whereby the Bible has lost its authority in society? Was it the rise of Darwin's evolutionary ideas that challenged the belief in God who made human beings distinct from other creatures? Should we blame it on the rising numbers of non-Christian immigrants? What about general apathy?

According to the Pew Research Center, "Between 2010 and 2050, the largest Christian population growth, in percentages terms, is projected to occur in sub-Saharan Africa (115%). However, the population growth of Christians in sub-Saharan African is expected to be less than in the region overall (131%). By contrast, population growth of Christians in Asia and the Pacific is projected to be higher (33%) than in the region overall (22%)."[3] Incidentally, demographers note that the rate of the world's population is expected to decline in the next few decades, falling from 1.1 percent in 2010–15 to 0.4 percent in 2045–50, with the annual growth rate of Christians expected to remain on par with world population growth.[4]

3. "Christians," Pew Research Center, April 2, 2015, http://www.pewforum.org/2015/04/02/christians/.
4. Pew Research Center, "Christians."

Researchers project that by the year 2050 the following numerical changes will occur in Christianity worldwide.[5] By 2050, Africa and the Latin America–Caribbean region will be home to more than six in ten of the world's Christians, with just a quarter of Christians living in Europe and North America. In 2050, nearly four in ten of the world's Christians will be living in sub-Saharan Africa, which means that the rate of increase has moved from 2 percent (1910), to 24 percent, to 38 percent by that year (2050). It is astonishing to think that the population of sub-Saharan Africa is expected to more than double between 2010 and 2050 (from 823 million to 1.9 billion). How will that impact the church?

In the Asia-Pacific region, Christians make up about 13 percent of the population; that percentage is projected to remain the same. In Europe, the number of Christians is expected to drop, in part because of people leaving Christianity (deconversion), the rising numbers of non-Christian immigrants, and other factors such as lower-than-average European birth rates. The number of Christians in Europe is estimated to drop from 75 percent (2010) to 65 percent (2050).

Finally, Christianity in North America is forecast to drop from 77 percent (2010) to 66 percent (2050).[6] Changes in the numbers of Christians in North America will be related to people leaving Christianity, immigration of non-Christians, and other factors. Demographers Todd Johnson and Gina Bellofatto note that the growth of Christianity in Eastern Asia will be the highest projected rate for Christianity, in part, they say, because of the comparatively small Christian population.[7] They also report that "Renewalists" (e.g., charismatics and pentecostals) are expected to grow at twice the rate of overall Christianity globally, and by 2020 will represent nearly 28 percent of all Christians worldwide.[8]

5. Numbers in this paragraph come from Pew Research Center, "Christians."

6. David Masci, "Christianity Poised to Continue Its Shift from Europe to Africa," Pew Research Center, April 7, 2015, http://www.pewresearch.org/fact-tank/2015/04 /07/christianity-is-poised-to-continue-its-southward-march/.

7. Todd M. Johnson and Gina A. Bellofatto, "Key Findings of Christianity in Its Global Context, 1970–2020," *International Bulletin of Missionary Research* 27, no. 3 (2013): 158.

8. Johnson and Bellofatto, "Key Findings," 158.

Surprising changes could be ahead. Who would have thought that China could have more Christians than the United States? That is what Purdue University sociologist Fenggang Yang argues, due to the massive growth of Protestant Christianity in China within a decade. Yang believes the numbers of Protestant Christians in China will swell to around 160 million by 2025, which would put China ahead of the United States, which in 2010 had 159 million Protestants. Yang states, "By my calculations China is destined to become the largest Christian country in the world very soon. . . . It is going to be less than a generation. Not many people are prepared for this dramatic change."[9] Rodney Stark suggests a similar future for Chinese Christianity: "If we accept that there were about 61 million Chinese Christians in 2007, then the rate of growth from 1980 through 2007 averaged about 7 percent a year. If that same rate of growth were to hold until 2030, there would be more Christians in China than in any other nation: 295 million."[10]

Yet an opposite story is being told in the Middle East, the birthplace of Christianity. In large part because of the terrible persecution of Christians by Islamist groups such as al-Qaeda and Islamic State, Christianity in several areas of the Middle East has declined dramatically to a fraction of its earlier numbers, especially in Egypt, Syria, and Iraq.[11] Ongoing violence against Christians in Egypt, the overwhelming majority of whom are Coptic Orthodox, has raised serious questions for the survival of Christianity, since national leadership and local authorities, such as police, judges, and business owners, "are infected with a rejection of Christianity."[12] Many Coptic and other Egyptian Christians have been abducted, killed, or forced to convert to Islam, particularly since the 1980s.

9. Tom Phillips, "China on Course to Become 'World's Most Christian Nation' within 15 Years," *The Telegraph*, April 19, 2014, https://www.telegraph.co.uk/news/worldnews/asia/china/10776023/China-on-course-to-become-worlds-most-Christian-nation-within-15-years.html.

10. Rodney Stark, *The Triumph of Faith: Why the World Is More Religious than Ever* (Wilmington, DE: ISI Books, 2015), 152.

11. It is important to note that "Islamist" differs from mainstream Islam. The vast majority of Muslims are "mainstream," while a small minority adheres to Islamist perspectives, which includes using violence to implement Sharia law.

12. Harriet Sherwood, "Christians in Egypt Face Unprecedented Persecution, Report Says," *The Guardian*, January 10, 2018, https://www.theguardian.com/world/2018/jan/10/christians-egypt-unprecedented-persecution-report.

While Christianity still exists in Iraq, the numbers have decreased so dramatically that Canon Andrew White, vicar of the Anglican Church in Iraq until he was forced to depart at the end of 2014 for security concerns, said that Christianity is over in Iraq. In 2003 there were approximately 1.5 million Christians in Iraq; today there are fewer than 250,000. The decline is mostly due to violence against Christians by Islamist groups that have singled out religious minorities, including some Muslims, for brutal treatment.

Syrian Christianity is one of the oldest forms of Christianity in the world. Some Syrian Christians still speak Aramaic, the language Jesus spoke. Since 2011, Syria's Christian population shrank from 30 percent to less than 10 percent of the population, driven out by Islamists. Church buildings have been converted into Islamic centers, and Christian leaders are targeted for abduction or attack.

Open Doors' World Watch List on global persecution of Christians notes that 260 million Christians experience high levels of persecution. North Korea, the most dangerous country for Christians, was ranked as the top country that persecuted Christians (since 2002).[13] The North Korean state is the primary driver of Christian persecution.

Open Doors reports that two of the major causes for Christian persecution are the spread of radical Islam and the rise of religious nationalism. Open Doors predicts that Southeast Asia is the next emerging hotspot for Christian persecution, fueled by Islamist extremism in Malaysia, Indonesia, the Philippines, and the Maldives.

Some early Christian growth was fueled by persecution, beginning with the scattering of Christians following the stoning of Stephen. Tertullian's adage "The blood of the martyrs is the seed of the church," which too frequently and indirectly celebrates the connection between harm done to Christians and the expansion of Christianity, fails to account for the many times when persecution destroyed Christianity. Think, for instance, of the history of Christianity in Japan, northern Africa, and parts of the Middle East. Christianity is not faring well in these locations. Consequently, while persecution

---

13. Open Doors USA, https://www.opendoorsusa.org/wp-content/uploads/202
0/01/2020_World_Watch_List.pdf.

sometimes stimulates Christian growth—such as in South Sudan—it is not universally accurate that persecution of Christians necessarily spurs growth. What persecution of Christians does seem to do is to bring unity of the persecuted.


## Internet Christianity

When my family lived in Grand Rapids, Michigan, we visited Woodland Drive-In Church, where the pastor used a handheld microphone to preach from underneath an overhang attached to a simple building, as parishioners listened via radio from the comfort of their own cars. Even on a snowy day, the church gathered, with tithes and offerings being collected by a person walking car to car with a container the size of a Kentucky Fried Chicken bucket. Drive-in churches were a feature of the landscape of American Christianity in the mid-twentieth century. In fact, in 1955 Robert Schuller began the famous Crystal Cathedral in Southern California with the first services held at the Orange Drive-In Theater. The drive-in theater combined a car-friendly service with the tradition of an outdoor service. These drive-in churches, some of which still exist today in the United States, were modeled on the drive-in theaters of the mid-twentieth century, reminding us that innovation has always marked the communication of the gospel. Christians have used almost every conceivable way and style of communication to convey Christianity.

Nowadays, however, we need to consider another profoundly important feature of contemporary Christianity that has been facilitated by the Internet: Internet Christianity. Enabled by the Internet, twenty-first-century Christianity, now more than ever, is a fluid religion liberated from the requirement of bodily participation in worship. The Internet has become a channel for communicating the gospel across the globe, and thus is changing the face of Christianity and expanding its growing edges. Christian identities are being shaped increasingly by ideas, sermons, theologies, worship, and products mediated by the Internet rather than through face-to-face engagement. This is a unique kind of "going," a movement that we need to take seriously.

In the last few decades, new spaces have proliferated, diversi-
fied, and been sacralized, providing "sacred spaces" across national
boundaries. The Internet collapses time and space, making personal,
embodied encounter unnecessary and disembodied virtual association possible. These online sacred spaces have put a new spin on
the idea that the church is not a building; it is the people. While the
people are real, their connections are disembodied.

Internet Christianity is replete with "apostles and prophets"
pushed through a network of content providers. What marks Internet Christianity is not a common physical space but rather mediated
relationships via the Internet, with the occasional attendance at conferences and ministry schools. In part because Internet Christianity
is composed of networks of dynamic leaders rather than congregations and denominations, the fissiparous movement might very well
represent a reconfiguring of the future of global Christianity.

With the decline of most forms of Christianity in the United
States, and the fact that the only Protestant churches that grew faster
than the overall population growth rate were the independents (e.g.,
independent evangelical churches, Bible churches, neo-charismatic
and pentecostal churches), there is good reason to believe that Internet Christianity will continue to be an edge of Christian increase.
Furthermore, social media and mobile apps, such as WhatsApp and
WeChat, are increasingly being utilized around the world for "cyber
fellowship," such as providing encouragement through Scripture and
prayer. These approaches will become more commonplace, particularly when there are illness-related issues, such as the coronavirus of
2020, that prevent people from assembling together.

As these Internet spaces are accepted as new neighborhoods and
cultures, Christian mission will increasingly speak into that space.
Christians have always employed whatever communication means
possible to convey the faith. The church is engaging cyberculture
and thinking about its engagement in that space. Cyberspace is a
disembodied space with twenty-four-hour access. Barna notes that,
in the United States, "nearly nine in 10 pastors say they believe it is
theologically acceptable for a church to provide faith assistance or
religious experiences to people through the Internet (87%)," and that
"today, just about half of pastors believe people will have all of their

faith experiences online within 10 years."[14] Church is a conduit for Christian online experiences.

Internet Christianity reflects an escalation of our late-modern societies marked by single-stranded connections, where relationships focus just on a single connection (say, disembodied worship) rather than face-to-face encounters at church. Face-to-face encounters can be described as multistranded connections, since they involve fully embodied presence with one another (physically, emotionally, spiritually). Internet Christianity has given rise to phantom-like transactions of digitally mediated encounters where our faces are two-dimensional or nonexistent, our voices modulated, our bodies vanished.

Yet Internet Christianity and the connections between Christians via social media appear to have benefits as well. In China, where Internet police keep a watchful eye on social media sites such as WeChat, the government has issued social credit scores for its citizens, based on the activities that the government disdains. The government looks at where one has been, one's friends, and how one spends one's free time, and then the government assigns a "trustworthy" score. One's social credit score can be lowered if one attends church or spends time with known Christians. A low social credit score can hinder one from purchasing tickets for planes or trains, and even restrict one's job opportunities. In response to the threat of censorship, a platform called DingDash was created to provide people with freedom of speech, religion, and ideas. Christians are using such platforms in restricted areas, enabling fellowship, learning, and encouragement in regions of the world with restrictive censorship. Digitally mediated fellowship might not be entirely negative.

## Future Issues

This chapter concludes with brief reflections on two topics that will impact the future of Christianity: human migration and the creeping abstraction of faith. First, we need to think seriously about the

14. "Cyber Church: Pastors and the Internet," Barna, February 11, 2015, https://www.barna.com/research/cyber-church-pastors-and-the-internet.

relationship between human migration and Christianity. Human migration will be a theologically defining issue in this century. As Christians cross borders, whether to flee violence or to seek better opportunities, they will take their understanding of God with them. Yet alongside all the changes that these Christians will encounter, they will also experience a change in their understanding of God, beginning with the most basic issue—the name of God.

The names for God are localized to particular regions. Yet, under conditions of migration, God's name changes. The Aguaruna of the Peruvian Amazon refer to "God" as Apajui in their local villages; in North Sulawesi, Indonesia, the Minihasa name for God is Empung; among the Walak Dani of the West Papuan Highlands, Indonesia, it is Walkagire; and for the Maasai of Kenya, the name is Ngai. Each of these local names for God carries with it characteristics, qualities, and expectations of each people's concept of God. These local names are connected to environmental features and life passages. For example, "Walkagire appears on that mountain." Missionaries understood those names to be God, as revealed in the Bible. Missionary Bible translations employed those local names for God to convey the gospel.

As people migrate to urban centers, those local names for God and the particular emphases conveyed through those names are diminishing. As Aguaruna migrate to Lima, Apajui drops out entirely from worship, since Apajui now becomes Dios in urban churches. Aguaruna children and grandchildren of migrants might not even learn the name Apajui after their migration to the city. Today, Minahasans and Walak Dani who move to Jakarta use the name of Allah to refer to God in their congregational singing, and Empung and Walkagire drop out entirely. Likewise, for the Maasai migrating to Nairobi, Ngai becomes Mungu (also Mulungu in Swahili) or God in English.

These linguistic shifts are happening all over the world, all the time, and they bear significant theological consequences that will shape the future of our understanding of Christianity. Indigenous names for God represent unique theological insights on the Divine. What are the theological implications of losing those indigenous names for God? What about particular insights and histories that will be forgotten through time? What happens when the name of God is torn apart from the land? What is gained and what is lost in such a grafting of the local onto the universal?

A second unique feature of the future of Christianity that we ought to keep our eye on is the burgeoning of a form of Christianity that Charles Taylor would call "excarnational." Taylor uses the term "excarnational," in contrast to "incarnational," to describe shifts toward disembodied faith, disconnected from physical and present sacraments. Excarnational gives priority to what lies in the head, dismissing the bodily and physical. Internet Christianity exemplifies the excarnational in that it denies the wholeness of humanity in the face of a disembodied spiritual life. What does it mean for the church to be the body of Christ when it is mediated by optical fibers and Wi-Fi rather than direct encounters with one another as a worshiping community? How might this excarnational approach reflect a new form of spirituality itself? It is not surprising that we also see countervailing movements that aspire to rescue the body, such as churches that hike together or share coffee together, to provide opportunities for believers to gain a sense of their full humanity—to seek incarnation.

The Internet is where the excarnational substitutes for incarnational presence. When coupled with commercialized products (e.g., worship music, conferences, books by celebrity preachers), Internet Christianity promotes a sense of virtual community through the purchase of shared commodities and associations (e.g., shirts, emblems, logos, celebrity pastors, worship bands).

William Cavanaugh raises concerns about such a view of the church, particularly when coupled with consumerism and the products we purchase from those spaces. What we purchase can create false community and, more troubling, lead to an ethics gutted of real engagement with the world.

> Consumerism is a spiritual discipline that, like other spiritual practices, lends itself to a certain practice of community. In identifying with the images and values associated with certain brands, we also identify ourselves with all the other people who make such an identification. Consumerism also allows us to identify with other places and other cultures through our purchases. White kids in Illinois can listen to reggae music and feel themselves in solidarity with the struggles of

poor blacks of Jamaica. As Vincent Miller points out, however, such types of "virtual" community tend to reduce community to disembodied acts of consumption.[15]

Vincent Miller further contends, "This abstraction impedes the translation of ethical concerns into action, reducing ethics to sentiment."[16] The Catholic Church's documents "The Church and the Internet" and "Ethics and the Internet" offer an instrumental view of the Internet as a means for spreading the gospel. Yet others disagree with what might appear as the benign nature of the Internet, arguing that the digital divide, the gulf between those who have access to computers and the Internet and those who do not, and the destructive potential of the Internet—for instance, the loss of culture and personal presence—should not be overlooked. The downside of Internet Christianity is that it reduces Christianity to "abstracted, virtual sentiments that function solely to give flavor to the already established forms of everyday life or to provide compensations for its shortcomings."[17] Internet Christianity produces shallow engagement with the teachings, the symbols, and the very embodiment necessary for Christian faith.

Where is Christianity going? In terms of its geographical spread, Christianity is growing in the Global South and Southeast, where extremes of wealth and poverty, minority and majority status, and relationships between Christians and non-Christians are raising important new questions about God, local cultures, suffering, displacement, and modern notions of the self. How will Christianity be reconceived as Christians living in hinterland regions migrate to urban centers? How will Christians understand God, the church, and their local traditions in those cities? Christianity is also flourishing in Internet realms, where cyber globalization will present new opportunities and challenges for the faithful. For all the good that Internet Christianity might provide—such as allowing Christians without access

15. William T. Cavanaugh, *Being Consumed: Economics and Christian Desire* (Grand Rapids: Eerdmans, 2008), 50.
16. Vincent J. Miller, *Consuming Religion: Christian Faith and Practice in a Consumer Culture* (New York: Continuum, 2003), 76.
17. Miller, *Consuming Religion*, 105–6.

to a physical church to feel some degree of connection with other Christians or providing Christian witness in areas with no Christian presence—what are the downsides of relying too heavily on digitally mediated experiences of the church? The answers to these questions will impact the future of Christianity.

Conspicuously absent in this discussion has been the placement of Christianity within the context of other major world religions. What Christianity is depends, in part, upon its relationship to its context. In the next chapter I will explore comparative themes between Christianity and other world religions with a goal of better understanding Christian uniqueness.

# 7

# How Does Christianity Relate to Other Religions?

O n a visit to southern India several years ago, a group of students and I spent a day at a Christian ashram, a place indistinguishable from Hindu places of meditation, except that the leaders, symbols, and chants were directed to the Triune God rather than to one or many of the gods of the Hindu pantheon. Traditionally, an ashram is a Hindu monastery or place of spiritual hermitage and meditation. Ashrams are important in Hindu tradition because they are places of spiritual shelter, where Hindus meditate and seek unity with the Divine. At the Christian ashram, we observed Christian monks chanting in Sanskrit to Jesus Christ, while sitting in a traditional yoga position. Near the entrance to one of the main meditation halls, I took a photo of a small statue of Jesus meditating in a lotus position under a grove of trees, replete with *tilak*, the mark on one's forehead that denotes a pious person.

Many Hindus are vehemently critical of any attempt to contextualize Christianity in Hindu cultural clothing, philosophy, architecture, and worship. The offense is not limited to those in India. At the 2002 annual meeting of the American Academy of Religion in Toronto, I watched as Father Francis Barboza, an Indian Catholic, performed the Hindu classical dance form Bharata Natyam in front of approximately one thousand people. Scandalous to some was that Barboza used the Bharata Natyam form not to convey Hindu worship but to present Christian themes. With a PhD in performing arts and degrees in philosophy and theology, Barboza has performed his imaginative dance in more than twenty-five countries, yet not without significant conflict. For many, Father Barboza's dance has pushed the boundaries of religion too far, thus causing heated debate and raising the ire of both Catholics and Hindus.

In India, the controversy about Father Barboza's use of Bharata Natyam was at times fierce. Swami Kulandaiswami of Maharashstra wrote, "If in the pseudo-spirit of inculturation and Indianization the bishops want to boost the dancing priest [Father Barboza] . . . they should not forget that it is only in the Catholic Church and in no other religion that we find such a ridiculous phenomenon."[1] According to a blog, "The Catholics hound him [Father Barboza] for dancing half-naked and for bringing pagan elements into the church, while Hindus frown upon a Christian stepping into their sacrosanct world."[2]

According to Swami Kulandaiswami, the debate between Hindus and Christians regarding Father Barboza's dance hinges on the historical and religious origins of the dance. The swami argued that the dance was confined to the Devadasis, unmarried women who spent their lives serving in temples and were often sexually and socially exploited. "Dancing," wrote Swami Kulandaiswami, "was never allowed in high castes and good families until recent times when art and culture received a fresh impetus and dancing was accepted as a popular art."[3]

Father Barboza, in defense, contends that Bharata Natyam can be employed as a dance form "with firm conviction that true to our heritage, themes from other religions could be assimilated into this an-

1. UCA News, "Controversy Stirs about Dancer-Priest Using Hindu Style," December 7, 1988, https://www.ucanews.com/story-archive/?post_name=/1988/12/07/controversy-stirs-about-dancerpriest-using-hindu-style&post_id=37318.

2. UCA News, "Controversy Stirs about Dancer-Priest."

3. UCA News, "Controversy Stirs about Dancer-Priest."

cient temple dance with excellent fluidity and rhythmic refulgence."[4] Barboza has been fascinated with dance since he was a young boy, seeing dance as prayer, a meditation where the dancer experiences God and tries to share that joy with others. Not everyone rejects Barboza's dance. In 1986, Father Barboza won the Presidential Award from the Indian government for his dance, Mystery of Redemption.[5]

Conflicts about the place of Christianity in society, culture, politics, and economics are not new. These debates have been raging since the beginning of Christianity, as early believers had to contend with how to relate to their Jewish past, Hellenism, Greco-Roman religions, state power, giving to Caesar and to God, and a host of other social and cultural topics about family relationships, dealing with idols and food offered to idols, and getting along with different people.

Christianity, as I suggested in chapter 1, is not pure, in the sense of being disconnected from culture or society. A helpful metaphor to envision what I offer about the relationship between Christianity and culture is that of an onion.[6] Some mistakenly think that we can discover a pure form of Christianity if we peel back the layers of culture that have built up around it, similar to attempting to find a seed or kernel in the middle of an onion. When we peel an onion we end up with an empty center; likewise, when we peel back the layers of culture in an attempt to reveal some gospel core, we find nothing. This does not mean there is no such thing as Christianity. Rather, the metaphor of the onion illustrates that Christianity is carried in culture—in this case, the essential elements being in the skin of the onion. Spirit and flesh are together.

In the lucid words of Lesslie Newbigin,

> Neither at the beginning, nor at any subsequent time, is there or can there be a gospel that is not embodied in a culturally conditioned

---

4. UCA News, "Controversy Stirs about Dancer-Priest."

5. For a critique of employing Hindu forms to convey Christianity, see Rajiv Malhotra and Aravindan Neelakandan, *Breaking India: Western Interventions in Dravidian and Dalit Faultlines* (New Delhi: Amaryllis, 2011), 113–20.

6. This helpful metaphor comes from Krikor Haleblian, "The Problem of Contextualization," *Missiology: An International Review* 11, no. 1 (January 1, 1983): 102.

form of words. The idea that one can or could at any time separate out by some process of distillation a pure gospel unadulterated by any cultural accretions is an illusion. It is, in fact, an abandonment of the gospel, for the gospel is about the word made flesh. Every statement of the gospel in words is conditioned by the culture of which those words are a part, and every style of life that claims to embody the truth of the gospel is a culturally conditioned style of life. There can never be a culture-free gospel.[7]

Attempting to discover a pure form of Christianity would be like trying to peel back layers of an onion, where each layer represents a segment of culture. The history of Christianity is replete with stories where a "pure" form of Christianity is communicated to the detriment of local people and their cultures. Do Christians diffuse their cultural understanding of Christianity or translate it? We need to be reminded of the simple but potent Christian affirmation that the gospel is always enfleshed, clothed in culture, neither spiritually disconnected nor phantasmal—"The word became flesh and made his dwelling among us" (John 1:14). There is no other way in Christianity; without this spirit and flesh incarnation, there is no Christianity.

When I teach new ideas to students, I invite them to learn not just by considering static definitions—for instance, of "religion," "love," or "sacrifice." While definitions are crucial, we can learn much more if we place those concepts into broader contexts. It is one thing to learn that "religion" might mean "a particular system of faith and worship" or that "love" means "senses relating to affection and attachment," but it is immensely advantageous to understand "religion" and "love" by putting them into the context of cultures, societies, economies, histories, psychologies, literature, and even cuisine.[8]

With this in mind, this chapter considers the important ways that Christianity relates to other major world religions, given the fact that

7. Lesslie Newbigin, *Foolishness to the Greeks: The Gospel and Western Culture* (Grand Rapids: Eerdmans, 1986), 4.

8. These definitions of "religion" and "love" come from the *Oxford English Dictionary*, the former at http://www.oed.com/view/Entry/161944?redirectedFrom=reli gion#eid, the latter at http://www.oed.com/view/Entry/110566?rskey=cZp9Wn &result=1&isAdvanced=false#eid.

Christianity is different around the world in part because of those religious contexts. Here I underscore some of the similarities and differences between Christianity and the other world religions, while highlighting the challenges of Christianity in the context of other religions.[9] The future promises to be more religious with Christians and Muslims making up the majority of the believers. For instance, Johnson and Zurlo report that "in 1970, 81% of the world's population belonged to a religion. By 2050, it will be 91%."[10] Furthermore, "in 1800, 33% of the world was Christian or Muslim. By 2050 it will be 64%."[11]

## A Multiscriptural World

Christianity is not alone in terms of having a scripture that guides, comforts, and teaches its followers. In fact, Christianity's Scripture is singular—it is just the Bible—compared to the number of scriptures in other major religions. We live in a multiscriptural world, where all major religions possess texts they affirm to be special (sacred). Sacred writings contain the writings and words of the founders, prophets, and exemplars of the religion. All claim to be without human origin; that is, they are from God, the gods, or a source or principle beyond the human realm. As such, they tell followers how to live, think, feel, and engage the world and countless other topics.

Hinduism is a family of indigenous religions of the Asian subcontinent rather than a clearly defined religion with one holy text, temple, beliefs, or practices. Because of its enormous diversity and

9. For a general presentation of such themes, see Charles E. Farhadian, *Introducing World Religions: A Christian Engagement* (Grand Rapids: Baker Academic, 2015); Timothy C. Tennent, *Christianity at the Religious Roundtable: Evangelicalism in Conversation with Hinduism, Buddhism, and Islam* (Grand Rapids: Baker Academic, 2002); Karl Joseph Becker and Ilaria Morali, eds., *Catholic Engagement with World Religions: A Comprehensive Study* (Maryknoll, NY: Orbis, 2010); Hans Küng et al., *Christianity and World Religions: Paths to Dialogue*, trans. Peter Heinegg (Maryknoll, NY: Orbis, 1986).

10. Todd M. Johnson and Gina A. Zurlo, *World Christian Encyclopedia*, 3rd ed. (Edinburgh: Edinburgh University Press, 2020), 5.

11. Johnson and Zurlo, *World Christian Encyclopedia*, 5.

long history, Hinduism contains the largest corpus of sacred texts, including the largest epic poem in world literature, the Mahabharata, roughly ten times the length of *The Iliad* and *The Odyssey* combined and five times longer than Dante's *Divine Comedy*. The list of Hindu sacred texts usually consists of the Vedas, Brahmanas, Aranyakas, Upanishads, Sutras, the Mahabharata, the Ramayana, and the Puranas. And most of these texts can be subdivided, containing several books within them. For instance, the Vedas consist of ten books.

Buddhism, generally divided among Theravada, Mahayana, and Tibetan, borrows many significant ideas from Hinduism (e.g., karma, duty, reincarnation). Buddhist scripture includes the Tripitaka, also referred to as the Pali Canon (Theravada), the Sutras (Mahayana), and Tibetan, Mongolian, Chinese, Korean, and Japanese sacred texts. Buddhist sacred texts consist of the words of the historic Buddha, wisdom from Buddhist faithful, philosophical insights, and teachings for monks, nuns, and ordinary believers.

The most popular Chinese sacred texts are those from philosophical Daoism (Dao De Jing or Tao Te Ching) and Confucianism (which consist of ten books, the most popular being the Analects). Traditional Chinese medicine has its roots in these Chinese documents, as well as the popular notions of *feng-shui*, *yin-yang*, and *chi* energy. The principal Sikh scripture, Adi Granth (Guru Granth Sahib), is considered by Sikhs to be a living guru (teacher) as guide and master for Sikh living. The Adi Granth comprises hymns, poetry, and teachings of the Sikh gurus and early leaders beginning in the sixteenth century.

Judaism affirms the Hebrew Bible, referred to as the Tanakh, consisting of Torah, Prophets, and Writings, which make up the Old Testament in the Christian Bible. Islam adheres to the Qur'an, with additional material coming from the Hadith, a collection of the sayings and actions of Prophet Muhammad. The main branches of Islam, Sunni and Shia, follow different Hadith, giving variety to Muslim interpretations of Islam.

All of the texts of the world religions are more than just writings. Scriptures are, at least, stories about the world, people, and the human problem to be overcome, and they offer techniques for doing so. Not all sacred texts have clear statements, for instance, about the creation of the world. Historical accuracy may not be important for the religious tradition. Understanding a religion empathetically requires trying to know it from inside the religion's own logic and sensibilities, whether or not one is doing a comparison or an apologetic.

For instance, communication about a historical act of creation is less important in some religions. Hinduism and Buddhism, in fact, have several creation stories that are not meant to be literal explanations but rather ways to convey wisdom from their traditions that could guide followers and order society. An example is the earliest Hindu idea of the sacrifice of a cosmic man, Purusha, which created all of life, including the four ancient classes of Hindu society.

There are many topics that are analogous across the scriptures, such as cosmology, birth, marriage, money, death, and the afterworld. These are notional similarities, for they are similar but not exactly the same among the religions. Of course, what each scripture says about these topics varies, but there are similarities as well. Even religions that do not have a sacred scripture—for instance, the countless indigenous religions in the world that worship deities and spirits—have oral stories that provide knowledge about the world, creation, and human beings.

In general, some religious scriptures advocate for a principle or cosmic pattern of the universe, within which one is to live. Live by this pattern, and you will live well, these traditions say. This is the case for scriptures in ancient Chinese traditions (Daoism and Confucianism) and ancient Hindu traditions (Veda, Upanishads). Each posits a pattern against which all things are judged, rather than a personal God who creates and sustains creation and cosmos. Each of the world religions sees their scripture in unique ways. The Hindu tradition divides their massive corpus of scriptures between those that were revealed by a divine essence (*shruthi*) and those that were remembered (*smriti*) and handed down in oral tradition. Early Hindu scriptures speak about the pattern of the universe, called *Rita* or *Dharma*, rather than a personal God.

Buddhism does not affirm scripture as revealed, since the aim in Buddhism is to wake up to experience the world as it really is—to penetrate the illusion (*maya*) of the material world—which is fundamentally impermanent. There is no such thing as revealed truth or knowledge in Buddhism. Wisdom is not revealed from outside of oneself. It involves waking up to what is already there. This is why "Buddha" means "Awakened One," and does not indicate God, prophet, or spirit. Therefore, Buddhist scriptures record the insights of the Buddha and other Buddhists who have gained enlightenment. To Buddhists, the Buddha was an extraordinary man, but just a man who had awakened to the way to overcome suffering. Buddhist scriptures, then, contain the wisdom and teaching of the Buddha.

The Qur'an is the sacred scripture of Muslims, and it claims to be, among other things, a corrective to parts of the Bible that have been corrupted. When passages in the Qur'an mention stories from the Bible, those Qur'anic verses are believed to be substituting what is right for what became erroneous in the Bible when the Bible was translated. In the Bible, for example, Abraham nearly sacrifices his son Isaac; in the Qur'an, however, it is Ismael who is nearly slaughtered. The Qur'an is "the divine speech becoming holy book."[12] It is the recitation received by Prophet Muhammad during the years 610–32 CE.

In Arabic, "al-Qur'an" means "the recitation." Muslims believe that the Qur'an is infused with divine power. It is specifically a revelation in Arabic, so it should be recited only in Arabic. The Muslim view is that there is only one timeless revelation by Allah's messengers through the ages, without any contribution of their own. Earlier messengers, such as Moses, David, and Jesus, culminating in Muhammad, are human beings, not divine but divinely chosen mouthpieces through whom Allah revealed "the religion" (*al-Din*), Islam, and thus the recitation (al-Qur'an) is authoritative.

In the Muslim view, then, Muhammad was the recipient of the Arabic words that passed through him untainted, the unadulterated voice of Allah. As such, the Qur'an remains the pure word of Allah, literally Allah's word descended (Arabic *tanzil*, "descent") into book form. Muslims believe that as Divine speech the Qur'an conveys divine law incarnated in the words dictated verbatim by the angel Gabriel to Prophet Muhammad. As such, the Qur'an cannot be translated

12. Gerhard H. Böwering, "The Qur'ān as the Voice of God," *Proceedings of the American Philosophical Society* 147, no. 4 (2003): 348. The Qur'an has been translated into some European, Asian, and African languages, such as Latin, Spanish, English, French, Urdu, Bengali, Hindi, Gujarati, Tamil, Turkish, Japanese, Chinese, Indonesian, Swahili, Hausa, Yoruba, and Dagbani.

without becoming an "interpretation." Yet the Qur'an has been translated into several non-Arabic languages, but mostly by scholars and academics rather than by Muslim clergy. Muslims tend to avoid translations because, in the words of Yale professor of Islamic studies Gerhard Böwering, "all translations are crutches."[13] Translations of the Qur'an, which are considered to be the work of human beings, diminish its sacred quality. All formal prayers in Islam must be said in Arabic, while the supplications that follow can be said in any language, thus safeguarding the meaning of the message in prayer.

The Christian Bible is Spirit-inspired, animated by God through its writers (e.g., 1 Cor. 2:13; 2 Tim. 3:16), whose personalities and qualities affect their writing. There are several different Christian perspectives on biblical inspiration, ranging from views that God told each biblical writer what exact words to write, as a process of dictation, to views that the Bible is simply a product of human invention, which makes inspiration meaningless. If you read enough of the Bible, you will recognize that the writers' personalities are a part of the text rather than the Bible being a word-for-word dictation from God to human writer in a mechanical manner. For instance, Paul tended to write longer, more complicated sentences, whereas Mark's sentences are shorter and full of action. The human writers of the Bible were not mere transcribers. What they wrote was inspired by God, with firsthand knowledge.

Unlike the Qur'an, where translation out of Arabic lessens, some would say eliminates, its sacred quality, the Bible is translatable; its message is meant to be conveyed in every language. No language or culture has a privileged vantage point in Christianity. That is why the Arabic Bible, Korean Bible, Malaysian Bible, and English Bible are all the Bible, possessing the same authority. Language accessibility was important to the biblical writers, who wrote in the vernaculars of Hebrew and Aramaic (Old Testament) and Greek (New Testament). The New Testament writers, for instance, did not write in classical Greek but rather employed the Greek of everyday usage, Koine, which was commonly spoken throughout much of the Mediterranean and Middle East.

13. Böwering, "The Qur'ān as the Voice of God," 348.

Of course, Christianity is not the only world religion with a scripture that is translated; yet, the scope and depth of translation distinguishes Christianity from other traditions. The Christian notion of translation goes to the very foundation of the faith, beginning with the most important affirmation, "God." The word "God" is translated into all languages where portions of the Bible have been rendered. The fact that the Greek word *theos* and the Hebrew word *yahweh* can be translated as "God" (English), "Dios" (Spanish), "Allah" (Arabic), and "Ngai" (Gikuku) affirms that "God" can be translated out of the original language of its writings. In contrast, the Sanskrit term "Buddha" remains in the translations of Buddhist scripture, and the Arabic term "Allah" remains in translations of the Qur'an.

Rodney Stark highlights accessibility as a unique feature of Christianity in relationship to other religions:

> Unlike most religious "texts" associated with other world religions, neither the Old nor New Testament is a compendium of veiled meanings, mysteries, and conundrums—there is nothing about the sound of one hand clapping. For the most part, the Bible consists of clearly expressed narratives about people and events. Although there are many theologically challenging passages (in Paul's letters, for example) and some deeply mystical sections, most of the stories are suitable for people of *all ages and cultural background*, in addition to which they are interesting! Consider the Christmas story or the confrontations between Moses and the pharaoh.[14]

Both Christianity and Islam hold to notions of descent; that is, truth descends from the Divine (God, Allah) to human beings. Yet the meaning of descent is different in Christianity and Islam. In Islam that descent refers to the word of Allah into a book, the Qur'an. This is why to defame or defile the Qur'an is comparable to slandering Jesus Christ: to Muslims and Christians, respectively, these actions would be utterly deplorable. In Christianity, descent refers to God's Word in the person of Jesus Christ (John 1:1–14). This is why it is ultimately more accurate and respectful to both Christians and Muslims to

14. Rodney Stark, *The Triumph of Faith: Why the World Is More Religious than Ever* (Wilmington, DE: ISI Books, 2015), 409.

compare the Qur'an with Jesus Christ rather than the Qur'an with the Bible. Although the Bible and Qur'an are sacred texts, and their comparison helps us to be better informed about both religions, it makes good theological sense to compare Jesus with the Qur'an, for both Jesus and the Qur'an are the descent of the word according to their respective religions, albeit with different messages.

That the Bible includes human features in its writing is critical to understanding Christianity. If one believed that the Bible descended, even was translated, without human mediation and without leaving the lasting mark of its human writers, that would be more of an Islamic way of understanding inspiration. That is to say, the role of the writer and translator is absolutely crucial to the communication of the Word made flesh. A disembodied vision of the Word (Bible) that descended unmediated, without flesh (writer, translator), is how Muslims see the Qur'an, coming directly from Allah, through the angel Gabriel, and finally to Prophet Muhammad.

How do Christians live in multiscriptural contexts? In academic settings, religious people are studying one another's scriptures. For instance, Cambridge University's Scriptural Reasoning program allows Jews, Christians, and Muslims to read passages from their respective scriptures together. Most of us, however, will not have the opportunity to study other religious texts at a university or with representatives of those religions. But it makes good sense, whatever one's religious tradition, to read other religious texts so that one can appreciate the unique insights of those religions and recognize their distinctive features. One might be surprised by what one discovers. For instance, in my teaching, I am often astounded by how many Christians know so little about Islam, even if they live in Muslim-majority regions. The same is true about Muslim, Hindu, Buddhist, Sikh, and Jewish knowledge of Christianity.

## Challenges of the Religions

Christianity emerged in a first-century Greco-Roman and Jewish context. As it expanded, Christianity met countless new ideas, cultures, and religions, which often challenged the faith to rearticulate itself. Christian theology was birthed as a result of these encounters, as the transmission of the faith required new rhetorical strategies to "communicate God" (theology). Throughout history, those encounters have provided Christians with an opportunity to think seriously about the fundamental categories of Christian faith.

The same opportunity invites us today. Worldwide our societies are increasingly marked by incredible plurality. There are over ninety languages spoken in the Los Angeles Unified School District alone;[15] New York City is home to as many as eight hundred languages;[16] in the United Kingdom, with the largest number of community languages, there are approximately three hundred languages spoken in London;[17] there are over thirty thousand Somalis, mostly Muslim, living in Minnesota;[18] there are reports of between 350,000 and one million Christians in Iran,[19] making up roughly 0.1 percent of the population.

Sociologist Peter Berger presented some of the major challenges to Christianity in the late twentieth century. Those challenges remain pertinent today: the mythological matrix, experience of emptiness, and nonparticular historicity.[20] To Berger's thinking, I will add my own reflections. In the past, religious encounters were mainly the result of immigration, travel, and print media (e.g., letters and newspapers). While these modes of contact remain salient, the Internet has enabled any number of possible gatherings. From the comfort of our own residences, we can effortlessly communicate with religious

15. "Los Angeles Unified School District," Los Angeles Regional Adult Education Consortium, https://laraec.net/los-angeles-unified-school-district.
16. Sam Roberts, "Listening to (and Saving) the World's Languages," *New York Times*, April 29, 2010, https://www.nytimes.com/2010/04/29/nyregion/29lost.html.
17. "20 Facts about London's Culture," Greater London Authority, https://www.london.gov.uk/what-we-do/arts-and-culture/vision-and-strategy/20-facts-about-london%E2%80%99s-culture.
18. Anduin Wilhide, "Somali and Somali American Experiences in Minnesota," *MNOpedia*, December 5, 2018, http://www.mnopedia.org/somali-and-somali-american-experiences-minnesota.
19. "2017 Report on International Religious Freedom: Iran," U.S. Department of State, https://www.state.gov/reports/2017-report-on-international-religious-freedom/iran/.
20. Peter L. Berger, "God in a World of Gods," *First Things*, August 1993, https://www.firstthings.com/article/1993/08/002-god-in-a-world-of-gods.

people and learn their ideas at any time. Such encounters have led both to a greater sense of civil society and to increased forms of religious fundamentalism.

Christianity is challenged by what Berger called the mythological matrix of Asian religions—that is, the fluid boundaries between the realm of human beings, gods, and nature. Post-Enlightenment forms of Christianity, following the intellectual developments of the day, erected boundaries between these realms. We, for instance, see ourselves as disconnected from the natural world rather than being a part of it, free to analyze and use nature as we see fit rather than recognizing our dependence upon it. Most of the Asian religions (e.g., Hinduism, Buddhism, Jainism, Shinto) recognize a plethora of divine forces: the world is full of gods and spirits. These forces are intimately connected to the human and natural world. The Hindu tradition says that there are 330 million gods, not saints or spirits but full-fledged gods, while also recognizing one Supreme God—usually called Brahman. Shinto, the indigenous religion of Japan, recognizes countless kami (spirits) that reside in the forces of nature, such as trees and mountains, as well as in venerated people and ancestors. They have the power to do everything from helping traffic run smoothly in Tokyo to influencing the course of natural and human events in rural Japanese villages. Kami live in the same world as humans and nature. One challenge to Christianity in this regard is a theological one. Berger correctly notes, "The first commandment [have no other gods before God] given to Moses on Sinai ratified a radical polarity between God and man, and it purged nature of all its divine mediations. Creator, creation, and creatures became separate, distinct beings."[21] To overcome this rupture, some Christians have acknowledged the existence of many spirits, yet they affirm only the one Triune God, who is above all other deities.

Another challenge to Christianity is the notion of emptiness presented in some Asian religions, where the boundaries between self, world, nature, and the sacred are obliterated. For instance, both Buddhism and Daoism offer deeply provocative insights on emptiness, one of the most challenging concepts in religious studies. They claim

21. Berger, "God in a World of Gods."

that all is one, thus erasing individual identity. This can be attractive since, in this view, there is no "I" to be offended. Japanese Catholic novelist Shūshaku Endō's book *Silence*, and Martin Scorsese's 2016 film with the same title, explored the silence of God in the midst of the horrendous persecution of Christians at the hands of authorities in seventeenth-century Japan. Endō's work is difficult to read because of our expectation that God is characteristically not silent. God's speech creates. Endō presents the fullness of Christian emptiness in the midst of the silence of God. This undoubtedly causes unease in readers anticipating a Jesus who is glorified rather than humiliated, as he is presented in the novel, remaining silent throughout most of the story.

The experience of emptiness presented in the world religions challenges Christianity. Escaping from one's increasingly busy, stressed-out life through meditation, seeking to empty one's mind of its distractions, has become popular. Forms of Christianity that emphasize "doing" (works, projects, tasks, grades) can be balanced by a sense of quietude—"Be still, and know that I am God" (Ps. 46:10). Berger asks, "How can the experience of emptiness be reconciled with the fullness of God and His creation? What is the relation between God's speech and God's silence? Does one precede the other?"[22] When we consider Christianity and emptiness, I would add that while Christians see Jesus as the light of the world, cannot God also be in the darkness and in the silence? Jeremiah writes,

> "Who can hide in secret places
>    so that I cannot see them?"
> declares the LORD.
> "Do I not fill heaven and earth?"
> declares the LORD. (Jer. 23:24)

The psalmist also writes,

> Even though I walk
>    through the darkest valley,
> I will fear no evil,
>    for you are with me;

22. Berger, "God in a World of Gods."

your rod and your staff,
they comfort me. (Ps. 23:4)

A third challenge to Christianity involves the concept of history—what can be called nonparticular historicity. That is, Christianity is a historic faith, whereas some other Asian religions lack historical particularity. Christianity focuses on the Triune God in real time and space, directing, sustaining, and relating to human beings and the natural world. The Bible tells the story of God's dealings with the people of Israel and God's incarnation in Jesus Christ. Jesus was a real human being, also fully divine. Jesus experiences hunger and thirst and sadness and joy. He bleeds real blood.

There is, in fact, a good deal of long-established written evidence for the historicity of Jesus Christ. Jesus is mentioned by Roman and Jewish historians within only a few decades of his death and resurrection. The earliest of Paul's Letters, which make up much of the New Testament, were written within twenty-five years of Jesus's death and resurrection. Around 92 CE, the Jewish historian Flavius Josephus referenced Jesus in his history. There were no major debates about the existence of Jesus in the ancient world. He was in human history.

What can be a challenge to Christianity is the idea forwarded by other religions that truth can be conveyed by nonhistoric myth. This is particularly the case with Hinduism and Buddhism. Most Hindu deities are preexistent; they did not enter into real history, and they did not need to in order to communicate truth. Language describing them is figurative.[23] Therefore, according to the logic of some religions, history is unnecessary as a vehicle to convey truth. How are Christians to make sense of nonhistoric incarnations, deities, and mythologies? What role do history and myth play in imparting truth?

23. For example, Vishnu is said to have ten *avatara* (incarnations): a fish, tortoise, boar, man-lion, dwarf, Rama, Prince Rama, Krishna, Buddha, and Kalki. *Avatara* means "descent" but not necessarily into real history, for *avatara* are appearances and do not need any historical basis for their truth. Shankara argued that Vishnu appeared "as if" human, so he did not share the same human flesh. Christianity, in contrast, teaches that incarnation means being truly embodied in human flesh.

## A Return to the Ordinary

To conclude, let us circle back to the classic description of Christianity as consisting of both transcendence and immanence. God is recognized as both transcendent and immanent, illustrated in the "Our Father" prayer, "Our Father [immanence] in heaven [transcendence], hallowed be your name" (Matt. 6:9). Transcendence describes an aspect of God—sacred, above creation, other than his people. God is also immanent—intimately present in the universe, our world, particularly through Jesus Christ, a member of the Triune God. Deism and docetism deny God's immanence. Secular humanism denies religious transcendence. Christianity affirms both.

Human beings are wired for transcendence, yet Christian tradition teaches that seeking secular experiences of going beyond the ordinary will never fully satisfy. In the seventeenth century, Blaise Pascal put it this way: "What else does this craving, and this helplessness, proclaim but that there was once in man a true happiness, of which all that now remains is the empty print and trace? This he tries in vain to fill with everything around him, seeking in things that are not there the help he cannot find in those that are, though none can help, since this infinite abyss can be filled only with an infinite and immutable object; in other words by God himself."[24]

Religions recognize that many people are restless. In fact, restlessness is one major reason for the appeal that Buddhist meditation has in the modern Global North. To those stressed out and anxious, Buddhism teaches techniques that claim to release practitioners from their attachments, helping to dispel their angst. Christianity certainly says similar things, such as "The grass withers and the flowers fall, but the word of our God endures forever" (Isa. 40:8). But Christianity refuses to reject the importance of the physical world. Buddhism, in contrast, sees the physical world as merely an appearance, an illusion (*maya*), which Buddhist insight (wisdom) helps to penetrate. Christianity, on the other hand, affirms the goodness of the material world. Creation is not an illusion; rather, it is the arena of our spiritual, emotional, physical, and psychological

24. Blaise Pascal, *Pensées*, trans. A. J. Krailsheimer, rev. ed. (New York: Penguin, 1995), 45.

lives. Although it is fallen and imperfect, creation is part of God's act of future restoration (Rom. 8:19–21).

With the incredibly rapid rise of Internet connectivity, the tendency is to dematerialize Christianity, living Christian faith by lifting ourselves out from ordinary embodied experience via electronic media, thus reducing face-to-face fellowship. Dietrich Bonhoeffer's *Life Together* reminds us that the church is the meeting ground of Christianity, where we live as the body of Christ, exercising our gifts through that body. Part of the reason for the turn toward the transcendent is that modernity itself has reshaped us so profoundly and offered substitutes for spiritual and emotional happiness.

Under conditions of late modernity, where "human flourishing" is stripped from its reference to God and lived faith within a community, people can couple Christianity with anything that smacks of the spectacular or celebrity, anything that might lift us up out of our ordinary lives. Secular transcendence refers to the attempt to transcend the body, suffering, and evil, without embracing the truism of "even though I walk through the darkest valley" (Ps. 23:4)—failing to see a God who is transcendent and immanent.

I appreciate Charles Taylor's words regarding the importance of the ordinary. I include them here at length because they contain a helpful counter to an overly transcendent Christianity that overlooks the immanent.

> There is an important human experience here, one which has been repeated again and again in modernity, and one which in itself, in spite of its doctrinal dressing, is very often profoundly positive, for it involves the rediscovery and affirmation of important human goods.
>
> What is recovered in these moments of return is a sense of the value of unspectacular, flawed everyday love, between lovers, or friends, or parents and children, with its routines and labours, partings and reunions, estrangements and returns. Now we can have a strong sense of rediscovery here even without having been carried away in an aspiration to transcendence, just because one can easily undervalue the riches of the ordinary in relation to more exciting or flashy achievements and fulfillments in life—a career full of conflict and adventure, or a passionate and dramatic love affair. (But perhaps these are exciting ultimately because of our yearning for transcendence.) And then our

partner falls sick, or suffers a near-fatal accident, and we suddenly realize what this love means to us. Much of our literature recounts the recovery of the unspectacular ordinary.[25]

Taylor's corrective is a call to a renewed appreciation of everyday relationships and experiences, to turn again toward the value of what is human in our lives, for "no form of transformation is acceptable that eschews what is human in our lives."[26] We are reminded that Christianity itself is about the ordinary, about returning to the "rediscovery and affirmation of important human goods" grounded in the God-given and permanent order.[27] This incarnational necessity of Christianity makes Christian faith and history unique among the religions of the world.

25. Charles Taylor, *A Secular Age* (Cambridge, MA: Belknap Press, 2007), 628.
26. Michael L. Morgan, review of *A Secular Age*, by Charles Taylor, *Notre Dame Philosophical Reviews*, October 8, 2008, https://ndpr.nd.edu/news/a-secular-age/.
27. Taylor, *A Secular Age*, 628.

# INDEX

Israel, 114, 116–17
lectionaries, 118–19
liturgy, 114–15, 127
Lord's Supper, 119–22
music, 124–25
Nairobi Statement,
   131–32
offering, 129–31
prayer, 126–28
preaching, 128–29
Reformation, 124

rituals, 112–13, 127
Sabbath, 117
sermon length, 129
song, 122–26
spiritual warfare, 127–28
Sunday, 116–18
teaching, 128
transcultural, 131
Wright, N. T., 96
writing, 62, 68
Wycliffe, John, 78

Xavier, Francis, 45

Yang, Fenggang, 139
Yoido Full Gospel Church,
   86

Zechariah, 123
Ziegenbalg, Bartholomäus,
   45
Zurlo, Gina A., 153